Aristophanes: *Cavalry*

BLOOMSBURY ANCIENT COMEDY COMPANIONS

Series editors: C. W. Marshall & Niall W. Slater

The Bloomsbury Ancient Comedy Companions present accessible introductions to the surviving comedies from Greece and Rome. Each volume provides an overview of the play's themes and situates it in its historical and literary contexts, recognizing that each play was intended in the first instance for performance. Volumes will be helpful for students and scholars, providing an overview of previous scholarship and offering new interpretations of ancient comedy.

Aristophanes: Frogs, C. W. Marshall
Aristophanes: Lysistrata, James Robson
Aristophanes: Peace, Ian C. Storey
Menander: Epitrepontes, Alan H. Sommerstein
Menander: Samia, Matthew Wright
Plautus: Casina, David Christenson
Plautus: Curculio, T. H. M. Gellar-Goad
Plautus: Menaechmi, V. Sophie Klein
Plautus: Mostellaria, George Fredric Franko
Plautus: Trinummus, Seth A. Jeppesen
Terence: Andria, Sander M. Goldberg

Aristophanes: *Cavalry*

Robert Tordoff

BLOOMSBURY ACADEMIC
LONDON • NEW YORK • OXFORD • NEW DELHI • SYDNEY

BLOOMSBURY ACADEMIC
Bloomsbury Publishing Plc, 50 Bedford Square, London, WC1B 3DP, UK
Bloomsbury Publishing Inc, 1385 Broadway, New York, NY 10018, USA
Bloomsbury Publishing Ireland, 29 Earlsfort Terrace, Dublin 2, D02 AY28, Ireland

BLOOMSBURY, BLOOMSBURY ACADEMIC and the Diana logo
are trademarks of Bloomsbury Publishing Plc

First published in Great Britain 2024
This paperback edition published 2025

A catalogue record for this book is available from the British Library.

A catalog record for this book is available from the Library of Congress.

ISBN: HB: 978-1-3500-6567-3
PB: 978-1-3500-6568-0
ePDF: 978-1-3500-6570-3
eBook: 978-1-3500-6569-7

Series: Bloomsbury Ancient Comedy Companions

Typeset by RefineCatch Limited, Bungay, Suffolk

For product safety related questions contact productsafety@bloomsbury.com.

To find out more about our authors and books visit www.bloomsbury.com
and sign up for our newsletters.

Contents

Illustrations

Preface

In outline, this study of Aristophanes' *Cavalry* is arranged as follows. Chapter 1 is a brief introduction to the theatrical context in which Athenian drama of the classical period was performed. Chapter 2 looks at the Athenian political and military leader Cleon, who is the subject of Aristophanes' *Cavalry*. The next six chapters (3–8) explore the play sequentially, each discussing one or more structural elements of dramatic action. Chapter 9 gives the reader an overview of modern reperformances of *Cavalry* and is followed by an introductory guide to further reading. Translations of ancient Greek are mine unless otherwise indicated, and the Greek text and line numbers for the plays of Aristophanes correspond to the OCT of N.G.Wilson (2007a).

The help of many people went into bringing this book to publication. I am deeply grateful to C. W. Marshall and Niall W. Slater, the series editors, for the opportunity to contribute a book on Aristophanes' *Cavalry*. I owe untold thanks to C. W. Marshall, whose unfailing patience, constant encouragement and stimulating criticism made this book possible; to the editorial and production teams at Bloomsbury Academic (especially to Sophie Beardsworth, Moira Eagling, Merv Honeywood, Lily Mac Mahon and Zoe Osman); to Roman Roth for his enduring friendship and for reading parts of the manuscript; to Ian Storey for helpful discussions of many aspects of Greek Comedy; and to Peter Thonemann for help with some hard-to-find items of bibliography. I met with generous help in securing permission to publish images from Dr M. Maischberger of the Antikensammlung in Berlin and Dr R. Di Pinto at the Musei Vaticani. I am thankful every day for the kindness and support of friends who helped me while I was writing this book – in no particular order, Dimitrios and Julie Malakos, Andra Thompson, Donnell MacKenzie and Amy Strizic, Romie Ridley, Shayla Schipper, Matthew Hodgson, Peter, Sarah, Alexander and Samuel Thonemann, Lawrence Hene, Ashwin Hajarnavis, Jacob Knopp and Arne Fors.

This book is dedicated to my father Christopher Tordoff.

A Note on the Spelling of Ancient Greek Words in English

In this book, Greek and Latin words are presented in *italics*; where it is necessary for clarity, the word is preceded by the notation (Gk.) or (Lat.). In the spelling of ancient Greek words, the macron is used to distinguish the long vowels eta and omega (i.e. *ē* and *ō*) from the short vowels epsilon and omicron (i.e. *e* and *o*): e.g. (Gk.) *orkhēstra*, meaning the dancing space occupied by the chorus in the Greek theatre, or (Gk.) *prosōpon*, meaning mask or character.

In English many ancient Greek words, especially proper nouns, have long been rendered in a Latinate or anglicized form, in which they are more recognizable to the general reader than a strict transliteration would be. For instance, the latinized 'Delphi' and the anglicized 'Athens' are more easily understood than the strictly correct forms 'Delphoi' and 'Athenai'. In such cases, spelling follows *OCD*. Names of persons and places lacking a dedicated entry in *OCD* are directly transliterated (e.g. Cleon's associate, and possibly son-in-law, is presented as Thoudippos not Thudippus).

A Note on the Play's Title

The play that is the subject of this book, titled *Hippēs* in ancient Greek, is usually known, in English, as *Knights*. Here, it is called *Cavalry*, a decision that requires explanation.

The traditional titles of most of Aristophanes' eleven extant plays derive from their chorus, a pattern that is repeated in the twenty-nine plays that are lost but not regarded as spurious (for a synopsis, see Silk 2000: 14–17). The original titles of many ancient Greek dramas are uncertain, but in the case of this play the title *Hippēs* can be asserted with confidence, for this is how Aristophanes refers to it in his play *Clouds* (554).

The meaning of *Hippēs* is ambiguous. Literally translated it means 'horsemen' and in ancient Athens could also be understood to refer either to a property class of men who (notionally) owned war horses, or to a unit of the Athenian army (i.e. the cavalry) who were largely drawn from that property class.

Aristophanes' chorus in *Cavalry* is clearly intended as a military unit, not a wider class of wealthy, horse-owning Athenians, nor simply a group of men on horseback. Several passages make this clear: at *Cavalry* 225 the chorus is described as 'one thousand men', which was probably the size of Athens' military unit of mounted soldiers, excluding mounted archers, at the start of the Peloponnesian War (cf. Thucydides 2.13.8; Spence 1993: 10); it is implied that they are young men of an age for active military service (270); and their first action when they appear on stage is to conduct military manoeuvres against Paphlagon (243–4; see Hesk 2007: 143–4 for more examples of the language of cavalry tactics in *Cavalry*).

The English title *Knights* derives from the Latin name for the play, *Equites*, which in Rome designated the Roman equestrian class or horse-mounted soldiers. In the study of Roman history, (Lat.) *equites*, meaning the equestrian class, is often translated into English as 'knights'. To the general reader, however, 'knights' connotes primarily three things:

characters from the pages of medieval chivalric romance; the class of land-owners and equestrian soldiers, beneath lords, in the medieval feudal system; or the highest non-hereditary rank in the United Kingdom's system of honours, none of which is much help in understanding Aristophanes.

In my view, the title *Knights*, while enjoying the convenience of scholarly tradition, is inaccurate and misleading. By contrast, the translation *Cavalry* preserves, without unnecessary confusion, the essential military character of the chorus, since many modern armies contain mechanized units (e.g. armoured vehicles) that are called 'cavalry', as well as ceremonial cavalry units of military personnel on horseback (for a similar view, but arguing for the title *Horsemen*, see MacDowell 1995: 80).

Abbreviations

ABV	J. D. Beazley, *Attic Black-Figure Vase-Painters*² (New York, 1978)
Add²	T. Carpenter et al., *Beazley Addenda*² (Oxford, 1989)
APF	J. K. Davies, *Athenian Propertied Families 600–300 BC* (Oxford, 1971)
ARV	J. D. Beazley, *Attic Red-Figure Vase-Painters*². 3 vols (Oxford, 1963)
Beekes	R. Beekes, *Etymological Dictionary of Greek*. 2 vols (Leiden, 2010)
Campbell	D. A. Campbell, *Greek Lyric*. 5 vols (Cambridge, MA, 1982–93)
Carey	C. Carey, *Lysiae Orationes cum Fragmentis* (Oxford, 2007)
Collard-Cropp	C. Collard and M. Cropp, *Euripides: Fragments*. 2 vols: vii–viii (Cambridge, MA, 2008)
DFA	A. Pickard-Cambridge, *The Dramatic Festivals of Athens*² (rev. J. Gould and D. M. Lewis) (Oxford, 1968)
D-K	H. Diels and W. Kranz, *Die Fragmente der Vorsokratiker*⁶ (Berlin, 1951–2)
FGrH	F. Jacoby, *Die Fragmente der griechischen Historiker* (Leiden, 1923–69)
Gerber	D. E. Gerber, *Greek Elegiac Poetry: from the seventh to the fifth centuries BC* (Cambridge, MA, 1999)

Henderson	J. Henderson, *Aristophanes: Fragments* (Cambridge, MA, 2007)
IG	*Inscriptiones Graecae*
LGPN	M. J. Osborne and S. G. Byrne (eds, vol. ii), *A Lexicon of Greek Personal Names: Attica* (Oxford, 1994)
Lloyd-Jones	H. Lloyd-Jones, *Sophocles: Fragments* (Cambridge, MA, 1996; repr. 2003)
LSJ	H. G. Liddell and R. Scott, *A Greek-English Lexicon*[9] (rev. H. S. Jones and R. McKenzie, with rev. suppl.) (Oxford, 1996)
M-L	R. Meiggs and D. Lewis (eds), *A Selection of Greek Historical Inscriptions*[2] (Oxford, 1988)
OCD	S. Hornblower, A. Spawforth and E. Eidinow (eds), *The Oxford Classical Dictionary*[4] (Oxford, 2012)
OCT	Oxford Classical Text
PCG	R. Kassel and C. Austin (eds), *Poetae Comici Graeci* (Berlin and New York, 1983–)
Perry	B. E. Perry, *Aesopica* (Urbana, IL, 1952)
Race	W. H. Race, *Pindar: Nemean Odes, Isthmian Odes, Fragments* (Cambridge, MA, 1997)
SEG	*Supplementum Epigraphicum Graecum*
Snell-Maehler	B. Snell and H. Maehler, *Pindari Carmina cum Fragmentis*. Pars 1, 2 (Leipzig, 1975–80)
Sommerstein	A. H. Sommerstein, *Aeschylus: Fragments* (Cambridge, MA, 2008)

Storey   I. C. Storey, *Fragments of Old Comedy*. 3 vols (Cambridge, MA, 2011)

West   M. L. West, *Greek Epic Fragments* (Cambridge, MA, 2003)

Titles of Greek and Latin works and their authors' names are those used in the Loeb Classical Library, where available; all others follow LSJ.

Aristophanes and Drama in Classical Athens

Aristophanes, a writer and director of comic drama, was an Athenian born close to the middle of the fifth century (i.e. *c.* 450 BCE); the exact year is not known. Over his career (427–*c.* 386), he wrote forty or more plays; eleven survive, along with over 900 fragments. Like all writers of Greek drama, Aristophanes composed plays in verse, to be performed, at religious festivals (discussed below), by a small number of actors (limited to three speaking parts in tragedy but with greater flexibility in comedy) and a chorus who sang and danced. The actors and chorus were elaborately masked and costumed and performed in a theatre with a space for choral dance known as the (Gk.) *orkhēstra*.

Athens' most prestigious theatre was the Theatre of Dionysus on the southern slope of the acropolis. Its impressive archaeological remains (including stone seating for over 15,000 spectators) date to the late fourth century and largely obscure our view of the smaller auditorium that Aristophanes will have known there; but a raised stage and a 'scene building' (Gk. *skēnē*) that provided a backdrop to the action were certainly present. The capacity of the Theatre of Dionysus in Aristophanes' day is uncertain, but it will certainly have accommodated thousands rather than hundreds.[1]

The Theatre of Dionysus was used for productions at Athens' premier dramatic festival, the City Dionysia (also known as the Great Dionysia). Aristophanes' surviving City Dionysia plays (*Clouds*, *Peace* and *Birds*) were surely performed there (at the City Dionysia there were dramatic performances by three tragedians and as many as five comic poets). It is likely, but uncertain, that the plays Aristophanes wrote for Athens' other major dramatic festival, the Lenaea (where there were performances by two tragedians and at least three comic poets), were also performed in the theatre of Dionysus; the latter include *Cavalry* (Aristophanes' other surviving Lenaea plays are *Acharnians*, *Wasps* and *Frogs*). In this book, the assumption is made that *Cavalry* was originally staged in the Theatre of Dionysus.

By convention, Aristophanes is termed a writer of 'Old Comedy', an imprecise expression, borrowed from ancient writers, that is used to distinguish his kind of comic drama from the later and very different 'New Comedy', of which Menander (342/1– *c.* 290) is the only surviving example. Old Comedy, at least as we understand it from the evidence of Aristophanes, was highly politicized (many of Aristophanes' plays can be read as protests against war), 'roasted' or outright vilified prominent people, and revelled in fantastical plots (like building a city in the sky in *Birds*). By contrast, Menander's New Comedy is a 'comedy of manners', combining gentler humour with social and psychological realism focused on the ups and downs of (fictional) well-to-do Athenian families.

When Old Comedy ended and New Comedy began, and what value there is in speaking of 'Middle Comedy' as a transitional period between the two, are matters than cannot be resolved on the available evidence and are beyond the scope of this book. However, using 'Old Comedy' to refer to comic dramas of the fifth century is uncontroversial. This makes 'Old Comedy' essentially a genre of the age of the Athenian Empire, during which Athens enjoyed enormous power and wealth but also suffered from chronic political instability due to protracted warfare and the volatility of its system of radical democracy. Most of Aristophanes' surviving works are products of the Peloponnesian War (431–404), twenty-seven years of conflict between Athens and the states of the Peloponnesian League led by Sparta.

In antiquity, the canonical poets of Old Comedy, other than Aristophanes, were Cratinus (active *c.* 454–423) and Eupolis (active *c.* 429–*c.* 411). Fragments of their plays and of over fifty more of Aristophanes' forerunners and contemporaries survive. The fact that plays by Aristophanes are the only fully extant examples of Old Comedy makes it difficult to appreciate the range of the genre. Aristophanes' approach, based on political satire, fantastical plots, 'celebrity jokes' and parody of tragedy, was not the only possible one and was not necessarily shared by all other writers of Old Comedy. For instance, Eupolis was known for writing humorous send-ups of Greek myths.

Old Comedy, like tragedy, was a genre of choral performance. There was a chorus of twenty-four young men, organized around a chorus-leader (Gk. *koryphaios*). They danced, sang, delivered speeches and participated in dialogues in a series of interactions with the actors and the audience. The chorus of a comedy was larger than the tragic chorus, which numbered fifteen in Aristophanes' day, and it fulfilled a greater range of functions. By the time of Menander, the comic chorus' role had been reduced to singing traditional songs at the end of dramatic episodes; but in Aristophanes almost all the chorus' songs are original lyrics, composed by Aristophanes, and the chorus' participation is structurally essential to just about every aspect of the performance. To illustrate, many of the elements of an Old Comic play like *Cavalry* are choral or include a significant choral component: this is most notable in the 'parabasis', during which the *koryphaios* addresses a monologue to the audience. Other importantly choral elements are the 'parodos', the song the chorus sing as they enter the theatre; the 'exodos', sung as the chorus leave the theatre; and the agon ('contest'), in which the chorus judges between two sides in a debate; not to mention duets sung with actors, songs separating dramatic episodes, and lines delivered in dialogue with the actors.

In ancient Greece, performances of drama were not purely for entertainment; they were also ritual acts performed at religious festivals, especially those held in honour of Dionysus, the god of theatre. These festivals followed a ritual calendar that positioned them in the winter and spring. The slower pace of the agricultural year in the winter allowed for the time needed to organize and rehearse dramatic performance. The small 'Rural Dionysia' were held across Attica around midwinter; the larger-scale Lenaea (at which *Cavalry* was performed), in or near Athens, later in the winter; and the Great or City Dionysia in Athens, in the spring. There may also have been performances of drama in the early spring at the festival called the Anthesteria.

Most of the financing of theatre production came through Athens' system of 'liturgies', essentially an irregular wealth tax imposed on the richest men in the polis. Liturgists were tasked with performing an act of public benefit from their private resources, either sponsoring a warship (a trireme) for a year (the 'trierarchy') or a chorus for performance at a festival (Gk. *khorēgia*). The choral sponsor (Gk. *khorēgos*) was, in modern terms, the producer.

It is not known how poets were selected to have their plays performed, but the responsibility lay with the archons, the highest-ranking magistrates in Athens. The 'Eponymous Archon', so called by modern scholars because the year of his office was named after him (e.g. 'the archonship of Stratokles' means 425/4 BCE, the year in which *Cavalry* was performed), made selections of poets for the Dionysia, and the archon titled the 'Basileus' ('King') chose poets for the Lenaea. Once a writer like Aristophanes had been chosen to write a play for a festival, he was assigned a *khorēgos*, who assumed responsibility for the organization (and most of the costs) of the production. The duties of the *khorēgos* included recruiting members of the chorus, providing a space for them to train, and even paying for bed and board during their training, not to mention supplying costumes, masks and stage properties, and a banquet celebration after the performance. One responsibility that did not fall to the *khorēgos* was finding actors: they were assigned to the production by the city and their expenses subsidized.

The writer of the play might also be the director (Gk. *didaskalos*), as Aristophanes was for the performance of *Cavalry*. Sometimes, however, a director would be brought in to train the chorus and the actors, as a man called Callistratus did for Aristophanes' earliest plays (the lost *Banqueters* and *Babylonians*, as well as *Acharnians*). It seems Aristophanes preferred not to direct his plays: more than half his surviving works are known to have been staged by another director: *Acharnians, Birds* and *Lysistrata* were directed by Callistratus, while Philonides directed *Clouds, Wasps* and *Frogs*.

Choral performance in Athens had an importantly competitive aspect. Every drama was staged, at its original performance, in competition against other plays. By the 430s there were prizes at the Dionysia and the

Lenaea for the *khorēgos* (producer) of the winning chorus, the best poet (i.e. the writer of the script) and the best actor. As a writer or director Aristophanes is known to have won with three plays at the Lenaea (*Acharnians, Cavalry* and *Frogs*) and probably one at the Dionysia, the lost *Babylonians.*[2]

The competitive intensity of choral performances is illustrated by the creation of victory records in the forms of inscriptions, dedications and monuments. For example, in the contests in dithyramb (a chorus of fifty) at the Great Dionysia, each chorus was drawn from one of the ten tribes of Attica, Athens' system of military organization, and competed against the other tribes in their category. The victorious dithyrambic producer was awarded a bronze tripod, which he could then dedicate on a monument built at his own expense, in or near the sanctuary of Dionysus next to the theatre, as an enduring record of the victory. Various sources attest the dedication of plaques commemorating victories in tragic contests, and it may also have been the practice for comic performances. The producer of a winning comedy at the Dionysia is known to have dedicated the 'equipment' (probably meaning the masks) from his production.

Such was the prestige of competition at the Great Dionysia that the festival was the occasion of more than just choral performances of dithyramb, comedy and tragedy. Before any performance began, there were two processions through the city with lavish sacrifices and feasting. The first involved a torchlit parade to the theatre. The second procession, held by daylight, was a vivid display of Athens' civic and imperial identity, with citizens, metics (resident foreigners) and delegations from the cities of the empire all participating. Once in the theatre, an ordinary spectator sitting high up in the tiered wooden benches would witness the ten generals (Athens' highest-ranking military commanders) pouring libations of wine to the gods, listen to announcements of the names of public benefactors, and watch as the tribute of the subject states of Athens' empire was carried into the theatre and ceremonially displayed to the audience. Below, in the seats nearest the *orkhēstra*, the spectator would see various men honoured with front-row seating (Gk. *prohedria*). Behind them but still enjoying a good view would be the 500 serving members of the council (the body that prepared business for the democratic assembly). Some seating towards the front would remain empty until, in another ceremony, the orphaned sons of Athenians who had died in battle were brought into the theatre, presented with a suit of armour gifted to them by the city, and invited to sit in front-row seats. In short, the Great Dionysia was both religious ceremony and a performance of Athenian political and cultural hegemony.

Much less is known about the Lenaea (the festival at which *Cavalry* was performed) than the Great Dionysia, but it was certainly not the international affair with the same emphasis on the empire that the latter was: representatives of the subject cities were not present, for the festival was too early in the year for safe sailing. Moreover, the insistence on Athenian citizen identity was not as great: metics (i.e. non-citizen residents) could be members of choruses and were allowed to sponsor choruses, things that were not permitted at the Great Dionysia.

The Lenaea shared certain features with the Great Dionysia: there was a procession and a pre-contest introduction (Gk. *proagōn*) of poets and performers, which will have given theatregoers an idea of what to expect from each play; but the scale of Lenaea performances was smaller. In Aristophanes' day, tragic performances were limited to two tragic dramas from two competitors, whereas at the Dionysia three tragedians competed, each with three tragedies and a satyr play (the latter was a humorous, mythologically-based drama with a chorus of satyrs, semi-human creatures with goat's legs and tails; the only surviving example is Euripides' *Cyclops*). Again, in Aristophanes' lifetime, the comic competition at the Lenaea hosted at least three comic poets, and probably usually five, each competing with a single comedy.

Cavalry, in competition at the Lenaea in 424 BCE, was the first play that Aristophanes directed himself and it won the first prize for comedy, beating Cratinus' *Satyrs* into second place and leaving Aristomenes third (with a play of uncertain title, possibly *Wood-Bearers* or *Sheath-Bearers*). Almost nothing is known about Cratinus' *Satyrs* or Aristomenes' play and no fragments survive.

Aristophanes' *Cavalry* and Cleon

The production of Aristophanes' *Cavalry* (424 BCE) was a satire directed against the politician and military commander Cleon at the height of his power and success. In *Cavalry*, he is represented by the character Paphlagon, a foreign slave 'tanner' (i.e. leathermaker), who has taken over his master's house, which represents Athens. The summer before the play was produced, Cleon had won a singular victory over the Peloponnesians at Pylos on the western coast of the Peloponnese (Thucydides 4.1-23, 26-41). He captured 292 enemy soldiers, who had become trapped on the island of Sphacteria, and brought them back to Athens as hostages; of these prisoners of war, 120 were Spartans, by reputation the finest warriors in Greece (Thucydides 4.38.5). Cleon's victory was a crushing defeat for Sparta and a blow to the fearsome renown of its military. In practical terms its effects were no less devastating to the Peloponnesians. Not only did it bring an end to their frequent invasions of Attica, since Athens threatened to execute the hostages in the event of any future incursions (Thucydides 4.41.1), but Athens kept Pylos as a base for attacking the western Peloponnese and for encouraging the Messenians to revolt against Sparta.

Cleon's triumph changed the course of the Peloponnesian War, which until this point had mostly run in Sparta's favour, with Athens enduring invasions, plague and rebellion among the cities of the Empire. After Pylos, Cleon was rewarded with Athens' highest civic honours: permanent rights to dine at the city's expense (Gk. *sitēsis*) in the Prytaneion (the state banquet-hall) and privileged seating in the theatre (Gk. *prohedria*).[1] To what extent Cleon deserved these honours, or indeed any credit for the victory at Pylos, was a matter of bitter dispute. The narrative of the Pylos campaign in Thucydides (who is hostile to Cleon) emphasizes the element of luck in the fortification of Pylos and in the defeat and capture of the soldiers on Sphacteria (e.g. 4.3.1, 4.55.3, 5.75.3).[2] And it was undeniable that the campaign at Pylos had been initiated by the general Demosthenes (not to be confused with the famous fourth-century politician and speech-writer), who like Cleon appears as a character in *Cavalry*.

In *Cavalry*'s prologue, Aristophanes jokes that the mask-makers employed for his production were too afraid to make Paphlagon's mask a true likeness of the man it represents (230–3), but he says he is confident that the audience will recognize him anyway.[3] The original audience of *Cavalry* can hardly have been anything other than fully familiar with Cleon, for he had been highly visible in politics for at least five years and probably longer.[4] But for the modern reader of *Cavalry*, the historical Cleon behind the mask of the slave Paphlagon is difficult to perceive clearly. At the height of his career in the later 420s, Cleon was both notorious and wildly popular. Yet history has preserved a much clearer flavour of his notoriety than his popularity, since most of the evidence is found in elite-authored and obviously unsympathetic sources. The voices of the very many Athenians who voted for him, agreed with his ideas and identified with him mostly survive in the historical record only indirectly and by implication.

Cleon son of Kleainetos of Kydathenaion

Cleon, son of Kleainetos, was an Athenian from the city deme of Kydathenaion (also Aristophanes' deme), where his family owned a tannery (demes were the fundamental political units of Attica under democracy, roughly equivalent to modern 'boroughs').[5] Cleon was probably born in the 470s; he had a son named Kleomedon, probably another son called Menexenos, and at least one daughter, name unknown.[6]

Cleon had already become politically influential by the time of the outbreak of the Peloponnesian War in 431. During the early years of the war, he opposed Pericles' policy of avoiding direct confrontation with

Peloponnesian forces on land and later Nicias' policy of pursuing peace with Sparta. He served at the highest level of military command in the four years from 425 to his death in 422, being elected general (*stratēgos*) three times.[7] In addition to his famous victory at Pylos, Cleon captured the cities of Torone (Thucydides 5.3.2) and Galepsos (Thucydides 5.6.1) in 422. He was killed later that year at Amphipolis in an engagement with Peloponnesian forces under the Spartan commander Brasidas (Thucydides 5.10.9).

In Athens' democratic assembly in the 420s, in addition to opposing moves towards peace with Sparta, Cleon promoted a policy of mass executions and enslavement of the people of subject cities that rebelled against Athens; this extreme form of punishment was narrowly avoided by Mytilene in 427 (Thucydides 3.49) but was visited upon Scione (Thucydides 4.122.6) in 423 and in part on Torone in 422 (Thucydides 5.3.4). Another notable policy of Cleon's was an increase in payment for jury service, a move that evidently enhanced his popularity with older Athenians, and inspired Aristophanes to write his play *Wasps* (422 BCE).[8]

This brief account of Cleon's life and career is about as much as we know for certain. Further details are available, but the historical evidence is less secure. For example, Cleon has been connected to the crippling increases to the tribute paid by the cities of the Athenian Empire in 425, with a denunciation of the cavalry for cowardice, and with reducing financial support for the cavalry.[9] The latter deserves some discussion, since it may have influenced Aristophanes' choice of a chorus of cavalry for his first play after Cleon's victory at Pylos.

The Athenian cavalry, of whom there were 1,000 (with an additional 200 mounted archers) at the beginning of the Peloponnesian War (Thucydides 2.13.8; cf. Aristophanes, *Cavalry* 225), came from the upper echelons of Athenian society, since the pasture, water and feed required to keep horses were scarce in the arid conditions of Attica for any but the very wealthy. Many wealthy Athenians looked unfavourably on Athens' democracy, especially that of the kind promoted by Cleon and other demagogues: it drained their resources through wars and wealth taxes and limited their political influence, since many officials were appointed through sortition and popular elections.

The cavalry was strongly associated with oligarchical sentiment, and their anti-democratic leanings were notably demonstrated during the oligarchy of the Thirty, in 404/3, at the end of the Peloponnesian War (Xenophon, *Hellenica* 2.4.2-34). Under the restored democracy, there was widespread hostility towards the cavalry among ordinary Athenians (e.g. Lysias 26.10; cf. Bugh 1988: 129-43; Spence 1993: 216-24), and a decree was passed reducing their pay (the decree of Theozotides, see Lysias fr. 130 Carey; cf. Stroud 1971: 297-301).

It seems that there was a similar case of antagonism between Cleon and the cavalry in the mid 420s. The evidence is convoluted, but both Aristophanes (*Acharnians* 6-8) and the historian Theopompus (*FGrH* 115 F93, 94) refer to conflict between Cleon and the cavalry. The cavalry's horse-keeping expenses were defrayed by a grant of public money, the (Gk.) *katastasis* (cf. Bugh 1988: 56-8). Cleon apparently reduced or cancelled this source of support, perhaps a popular measure with many Athenians but obviously unpopular with the aristocratic cavalry class (cf. Bugh 1988: 112-14; Fornara 1973). The political battle over financial support for the cavalry is probably behind *Acharnians* 6, which speaks of the cavalry forcing Cleon to 'vomit up five talents'; the five talents would then be the restored *katastasis*. It has also been suggested that, in retaliation, leading members of the cavalry helped to prosecute Cleon for accepting bribes (Carawan 1990) and Theopompus (cited above) reports that Cleon accused the cavalry of desertion. In short, the cavalry were not only natural enemies of a politician like Cleon but perhaps also his aggrieved adversaries and therefore a particularly suitable choice for the chorus of a play about him.

A curious lacuna in the life of Cleon is the fact that, despite the existence of numerous pieces of evidence, we know very little about his family background. Cleon's father Kleainetos might be the same man as the producer (Gk. *khorēgos*) of a victorious dithyrambic performance by the men of the tribe Pandionis. A record of this victory appears in a fragment of a stone inscription recording the results in the competitions at the City Dionysia.[10] Cleon's deme, Kydathenaion, belonged to the tribe Pandionis, and no other man called Kleainetos of that tribe is known in the period in question, so it is probable that the Kleainetos in this inscription is Cleon's father.

The significance of this information is the exceptional wealth of Cleon's family. Producing a performance of men's dithyramb at the City Dionysia was extremely costly. The dithyrambic chorus numbered fifty, and each member had to be trained and costumed at great expense. In a speech written by Lysias (21.2), we are told that in 409 BCE a producer, whose name is unknown, spent 5,000 drachmas on such a performance, including the cost of setting up a tripod as a victory monument. Even allowing for some exaggeration (the speaker is clearly playing up his generosity to the city), this is a vast sum of money (an Athenian craftsman probably earned about a drachma a day; he would, therefore, take more than thirteen years, working every day, to make as much). If the Kleainetos named in the inscription is indeed Cleon's father, then their family belonged among the wealthiest in Athens.[11]

Most of our sources (primarily Aristophanes' plays and Thucydides' *History of the Peloponnesian War*) are hostile to Cleon. The only description of Cleon from classical Athens that is not appears in a law-court speech from the years soon after the middle of the fourth century. The speaker Mantitheos refers to his mother's first marriage, which was to Kleomedon son of Cleon and ended when she was widowed.

> ...and my mother is shown to have been given in marriage first to Kleomedon, whose father Cleon, they say, led your ancestors as a general, and in Pylos captured many of the Spartans and was held in the greatest esteem of all the men in the city.
>
> [Demosthenes] 40.25

This text is exceptional in presenting Cleon in favourable terms. The speaker is attempting to convince the jury that his mother must have brought a dowry into her marriage with his father Mantias, since she had previously been married to Cleon's son Kleomedon: such an alliance could not possibly have been made without a dowry because of the wealth and status of Cleon's family. This speech will have been delivered before a jury of hundreds of Athenian citizens, and it will not have been in Mantitheos' interests to risk alienating them by trying to present Cleon as a famous war hero, 'held in the greatest esteem of all the men in the city', if he had been generally held to be disastrous and disreputable, as numerous sources present him.[12] Clearly, Cleon's reputation among Athenians some seventy or more years after his death was quite impressive. This implies that he was more respected in life than Aristophanes, Thucydides, Plutarch and others would have their readers believe.

Cleon and Thucydides

Compare Mantitheos' speech (quoted above) to Thucydides' account (5.10.9) of how Cleon died at Amphipolis in 422:

> Cleon, since he, from the outset, was not intending to remain in position, immediately fled; he was caught by a Myrkinian peltast and died.

Thucydides' description of Cleon's death is pointedly discreditable, as is his whole account of Cleon (see Woodhead 1960). Not only does Cleon show cowardice and flee, but he is killed by a Thracian peltast (i.e. a barbarian armed with an animal-hide shield and a javelin), not a bronze-armoured Peloponnesian hoplite (contrast the account in Diodorus Siculus 12.74.2, which implies that Cleon and the famous Spartan commander Brasidas, who was killed in the same battle, died with equal heroism). Similarly, Cleon's great success at Pylos is emphatically described as a result of luck rather than good judgement (4.27.1–39.4): Thucydides assesses Cleon's promise to the assembly to capture the Peloponnesian troops on Sphacteria within twenty days with the words 'mad though it was, it succeeded' (4.39.3).

It is possible that Thucydides had personal reasons for disliking Cleon, for Cleon may have had something to do with Thucydides' exile from Athens in 424.[13] Yet whatever personal interactions Thucydides and Cleon might have had, the historian has shaped his account to present Cleon as the cardinal example of what began to go wrong in Athenian politics after the death of Pericles in 429. Thucydides' general assessment of the evolution of Athenian political discourse during the Peloponnesian War argues that Pericles' death created a political vacuum that no leader could fill; the result was a 'race to the bottom' among rivals in populism, which led to instability in policy and disastrous strategic errors (Thucydides 2.65.10-11):

> But politicians after Pericles, who were more on a level with one another, each aiming individually to become predominant, resorted for the sake of popularity even to giving control of affairs to the demos. The results of this, in a large city with an empire to rule, were many policy errors ...

Thucydides does not pretend to write a biography of Cleon but neither does he offer a balanced view of Cleon's career. Instead, he presents unflattering vignettes and is clearly high selective about what he includes and excludes: for instance, we learn nothing about Cleon's political opposition to Pericles, and the record of Cleon's death, as we have seen, includes details that a more sympathetic source might have omitted.[14]

In Thucydides, Cleon bursts on to the scene in 427, in the immediate aftermath of the revolt of Mytilene, an important subject city in the Athenian Empire. Thucydides presents Cleon at the centre of a fractious and bloodthirsty dispute in the assembly (3.36-41): Cleon had successfully carried a proposal for the mass execution of all the men of Mytilene and the enslavement of the women and children (3.36.2), but his opponents had managed to reconvene the assembly the following day to debate the issue afresh. Cleon is presented trying to defend his hardline policy towards rebellious subject cities against opponents who appeal for clemency. The picture is of an assembly sharply divided in its support for different leaders and easily swayed by sophisticated rhetoric. Thucydides' first description of Cleon is especially memorable (3.36.6):

> ... Cleon son of Kleainetos ... was in general the most aggressive of the citizens and at that time by far the most influential with the people.[15]

An interesting aspect of Cleon's speech in the debate over Mytilene is his attitude towards the Athenian assembly. He is pointedly critical of the assembly's ability to rule an empire effectively and its susceptibility to rhetoric, and he makes a political virtue out of ordinary thought and a lack of expertise (Thucydides 3.37.4):

> The simpler folk, for the most part, live better in political communities when compared to the more sophisticated. For the latter desire to appear intellectually superior to the laws and to get the best of public debate continually ... because of which they usually cause their cities to fail. But the former, lacking confidence in their own acumen, are prepared to be less educated than the laws, less able to criticize the words of a fine speaker, and being impartial judges rather than contestants, they more frequently prosper.

Cleon's professed anti-intellectualism and his enthusiasm for political decision making based on the collective wisdom of ordinary citizens rather than the technical expertise of a few experienced men appear elsewhere as features of his political strategy. The portrait that emerges is of a career built on being a 'man of the people'.

The author of the Aristotelian *Constitution of the Athenians*, who probably wrote several generations after Cleon's death, distills Athenian political history in the century after the foundation of democracy (509/8 BCE) into a series of oppositions between populist leaders who represented the interests of the people and aristocratic leaders who relied on inherited wealth and illustrious family histories of political achievement. The writer contrasts Xanthippus, Pericles' father, with Miltiades; Themistocles with Aristides; Ephialtes with Cimon; Pericles with Thucydides son of Melesias (a different man from the famous historian); and Cleon with Nicias. It is only on reaching Cleon that the writer pauses to describe the political style and influence of the leaders thus far listed ([Aristotle] *Constitution of the Athenians* 28.3). In describing Cleon, he writes:

> ... Cleon the son of Kleainetos represented the people ... he seems most of all to have corrupted the people with his attacks, and he was

the first to shout on the speaker's platform and to use abusive language and to address the assembly wearing his tradesman's belt, while the others all spoke in a decent fashion.[16]

The writer lists Cleon as Pericles' successor as a representative of the people but sees his political style marking a sharp degradation in the management of public affairs. The description of Cleon adds detail to a comment the same writer makes a little earlier about the decline of Athenian politics after Pericles' death ([Aristotle] *Constitution of the Athenians* 28.1):

> Then for the first time the people took a leader [i.e. Cleon] who was not well thought of among respectable men . . .

The clear implication is that Cleon began to do things that no political leader, neither popular nor aristocratic, had done before: he positioned himself as a man *of the people*, not just a man *for the people* (Plutarch, *Demetrius* 11.2 refers to Cleon's well-known 'familiarity' towards the people). While it may be objected that if we knew more about Pericles' early political career (see Plutarch, *Pericles* 7.2-3, with which compare the anecdote about Cleon in *Moralia* 806f-807a), we might see Cleon's as not so different, the description of Cleon's conduct in the assembly is unusually detailed and personal and no evidence directly contradicts the view of Cleon as a genuine political radical.

Aristophanes and Cleon

There are various explanations for Aristophanes' hostility towards Cleon; for, beyond the comic potential for ridiculing all people who possess authority and the eccentricity of Cleon's untraditional political style, there is scope for thinking that Aristophanes held a more personal antipathy towards Cleon. Aristophanes' personal dislike for Cleon (discussed below) was so great that the comic dramatist claimed to have invented with *Cavalry* the 'demagogue comedy', a new sub-genre of Old Comedy, of which he was immensely proud (cf. *Wasps* 1029–37; *Peace*

748–61): that is, a play focused on a single prominent politician. Most of the evidence for this relies on Aristophanes' own boasts in *Clouds* (549–62) partially quoted here:

> First of all, the despicable Eupolis despicably dragged on stage his play *Maricas* rehashing my *Cavalry*, topping it off with a drunken old hag doing the can-can . . .
>   Then again, Hermippus wrote a play about Hyperbolus, and now all the others are writing about Hyperbolus, copying my very own similes about eels! Well, whoever laughs at these plays, better find no pleasure in mine! But if you take joy in me and my inventions, in after years you will be held to have shown good sense.
>
> (Aristophanes, *Clouds* 553–5, 557–62)

Aristophanes complains that other comic poets copied *Cavalry* by writing plays about the demagogue Hyperbolus; he mentions the dramatists Eupolis, with his play *Maricas*, and Hermippus, with *Bakery-Women*, as the thieves of his invention.[17]

Making fun of prominent politicians in Old Comedy was nothing new. Aristophanes' complaints about Eupolis and Hermippus are almost certainly exaggerated: indeed, the comic poet Plato (not to be confused with the famous philosopher) claims that he made war on Cleon before Aristophanes did (fr. 115 Storey), and the ancient commentary on *Clouds* (Σ 557) says that Hermippus' *Bakery-Women* was not actually all about Hyperbolus (i.e. it was not really a 'demagogue comedy'). Yet the fact remains that before *Cavalry* no comic drama is known to have staged a central character representing a leading political figure in quite the way that Aristophanes did in *Cavalry* with Cleon as the slave Paphlagon.

It is not known when or how the antipathy that Aristophanes expresses towards Cleon began, and even the reality of Aristophanes' animosity has been questioned. Different factors, political, personal and poetic, could have had a bearing. The simple fact of Cleon's status as one of the most powerful men in Athens in the mid 420s made him a likely – if not inevitable – target for personal ridicule on the comic stage. His political views and tactics were no doubt objectionable to many Athenians, especially the wealthy elite. We might point to various aspects of Cleon's career that we have already mentioned, such as his opposition to peace with the Peloponnesians, his demands for harsh treatment of the cities of the Athenian Empire, his cultivation of a loyal base of poorer, older supporters through increased jury-pay, and his demagogic rhetoric.

But it seems that there was greater bitterness to Aristophanes' relationship to Cleon than that inspired by a difference of political views. Several passages in *Acharnians* (e.g. 377–82, 502–8, 515–16) imply that Cleon attempted to bring a prosecution against Aristophanes for some things that were said about the city in *Babylonians* (427/6 BCE). The point at issue seems to be that since *Babylonians* was performed at the Dionysia, foreigners, especially representatives from the cities of the Athenian Empire, had been present in the theatre when derogatory things were said on stage about Athens. The nature of the charges is uncertain, but according to the ancient evidence they included ridiculing Cleon, various officials and the demos (i.e. the people).[18] It is no more than a guess, but presumably Cleon suggested to the Council that *Babylonians* risked inciting rebellion in the subject states of the Athenian Empire. This was a very serious issue and one in which Cleon had experience: he had recently played a large role in the punishment of the revolt of the city of Mytilene (see above). Subsequent relations between the two men were hostile, with Cleon perhaps threatening or bringing further legal action.

Later, in *Acharnians* (425 BCE), Aristophanes challenges Cleon to do his worst (659–64), suggesting that any accusations over *Babylonians* failed to stick. The ancient commentary on the play (Σ *Acharnians* 378) records that Cleon took up the challenge and tried to prosecute Aristophanes again, this time for the production of *Acharnians*; however, there is no independent evidence for this, and it is strange that we do not hear about it in *Cavalry* in which Cleon (as Paphlagon) plays such a major role.

Again, in *Wasps* (422 BCE) there is a reference to a hearing resulting in a deal with Cleon (*Wasps* 1284–91) – a deal on which Aristophanes says he reneged.[19] Unfortunately, the verses immediately preceding this passage have been lost, which makes it impossible to establish the full context. One explanation is that the passage simply refers to the original dispute over *Babylonians* (Halliwell 1980: 35n.11). Or if Aristophanes is speaking of a subsequent legal action by Cleon, perhaps he made an agreement to avoid further denunciations and later broke his word. What caused Cleon to prosecute Aristophanes again is not certain, but the performance of *Cavalry* is the most obvious possibility (and there is notably little said about Cleon in *Clouds* in 423 BCE).[20]

Since the evidence for Cleon's accusations and subsequent events derives mostly from comic texts and the ancient commentaries on them, it has been doubted whether the episode is real; indeed, it has been suggested that it might be pure comic fantasy. This alternative explanation for Aristophanes' attitude to Cleon is entirely poetic (Rosen 1988: 63–4.). Iambic poetry, of which comic drama was one form, had a long literary ancestry, including poets like Archilochus and Hipponax. It was a convention of iambic poetry that the poet had an enemy, who was the target of his iambic ridicule (Lykambes for Archilochus, for example). In the same way, then, the argument runs, Aristophanes made Cleon his great and dangerous (literary) enemy, who was so stung by his plays that he took him to court – a stage fiction well understood by the audience and enjoyed no less for its fictional quality. On the state of the evidence, this hypothesis cannot be disproved, but it is well to remember that even if Aristophanes had invented 'Cleon' as his iambic enemy, there was nothing to prevent Cleon from becoming his enemy in real life.

Did Cleon really threaten Aristophanes with prosecution or not? Reliable independent evidence is lacking, but Athens was a litigious society and Aristophanes' attitude towards Cleon is exceptional. The chorus of *Acharnians* expresses *hatred* for Cleon – an emotion that is not very frequent in Aristophanes and one that he does not direct at any historical individual other than Cleon.[21] Furthermore, even after Cleon's death Aristophanes attacks him on multiple occasions in *Peace* (268–72;

313–15; 647–56; 753–8), more than he attacks any living public figure mentioned in that play (Sommerstein 1985: 47). Even more surprisingly, Cleon is mentioned unfavourably twice in *Frogs*, some seventeen years after his death. In general, mentions of historical events and persons in Aristophanes either belong to a topical recent past of about a decade or to a distant 'golden age' ending about forty years before the play was composed. The fact that Cleon is still the target of Aristophanes' barbs nearly two decades after his death seems indicative of a particular animosity towards him, and reference to his fondness for prosecutions (*Frogs* 577) might be inspired by Aristophanes' experiences at the hands of Cleon in the 420s. On the state of the evidence, it is not possible to rule out the argument that Aristophanes' struggle with Cleon was purely fictional – pursued only on the stage and motivated by the generic and conventional traditions of Greek iambic poetry. Yet the especially toxic vitriol directed at Cleon, even after his death, suggests that Aristophanes' hatred for Cleon was genuine and personal.

It has also been proposed (Lind 1991: esp. 87–159) that there was a local cause behind Aristophanes' antagonism towards Cleon. Aristophanes and Cleon came from the same deme, Kydathenaion, which was located inside the city walls to the north of the acropolis (for a map, see Figure 1). The argument is that Cleon's tannery was situated in Kydathenaion and was polluting a watercourse, the stream called the Eridanos, on which a cult site of Heracles was located; some likely associates of Aristophanes are known from epigraphic evidence to have been members of the cult (*IG* ii^2 2343; Dow 1969).[22] If the cult site was downstream from Cleon's tannery, the effluent would have polluted the lustral water used by the cult for ritual purification and angered its members. The same problem is known to have affected a cult of Heracles outside the city walls at Kynosarges on the river Illisos. The evidence for this derives from an inscription (*IG* i^3 257) dating to approximately 440–430 BCE, which bans the use of the Illisos upstream of the precinct of Heracles for softening hides, tanning and washing away waste products. The inscription appoints the Archon Basileus, Athens' chief religious magistrate, to supervise the placing of a stone marker on either side of the stream – presumably to mark the point above which water-polluting activities are banned.

If Cleon had caused a local dispute in Kydathenaion over the effluent from his leather-making business, it would help to explain the numerous references in Aristophanes to Paphlagon as a tanner. Hypothetically, then, we might imagine a dispute between Cleon and the members of the cult of Heracles over the use of the Eridanos, in which, perhaps, Cleon used his influence to try to prevent the kind of regulation that was used outside the city on the Illisos. The theory that Aristophanes and his friends and associates quarreled with Cleon over the effluent from his tannery is attractive but tenuous: it is surprising, if the pollution of the Eridanos was such a significant issue, that among the numerous references in *Cavalry* to Cleon's trade, there is no mention of the stream. But perhaps the matter had already been resolved by the time Aristophanes wrote *Cavalry*, and Cleon had already moved his tanning business elsewhere.

In summary, Cleon was very popular and powerful in Athens in the 420s. He defied tradition by fashioning his public image as an ordinary hardworking tradesperson, not a sophisticated, wealthy aristocrat; he pursued a new, risky and aggressive strategy against Sparta and the Peloponnesian League; possibly, to fund Athens' military exploits, he brought heavy new taxes on the Delian League allies and may have restricted the grant for Athens' cavalry. He may also have prosecuted Aristophanes and made himself unpopular in Aristophanes' deme because of his tannery. If Cleon's political style and actions represented a break from the ways of the past, it is hardly surprising that more conservative, aristocratic Athenians detested him, his business and his political successes.

In general, modern assessments of Cleon have followed those of Thucydides, Aristophanes, Plutarch and others. But as we have already seen, a fourth-century reference to Cleon in a lawcourt speech presents the demagogue in a more favourable light than might have been expected on the basis of the sources otherwise available. Another piece of fourth-century evidence merits consideration. In the *Rhetoric*

(1408b25), Aristotle observes that when slaves in Athens were freed by public proclamation and the crier asked, 'Whom does the one being freed choose as a patron?', the children would shout out 'Cleon!' Aristotle must have witnessed this more than fifty years after Cleon's death, so it was clearly a long-standing joke passed down in an oral tradition.[23]

A passage in *Frogs* might be related. Aristophanes makes a joke out of a deceased barmaid in the Underworld threatening to summon her patron, who is none other than Cleon (*Frogs* 569). Deciding how to explain why the children's cry of 'Cleon' became traditional is difficult. Had Cleon made a habit of freeing slaves and acting as their legal repesentative, as Athenian law required, to the point that his name had become a frequent response to the crier's question? Or was it merely a joke, suggesting that the lowest levels of Athenian society would naturally gravitate to a man like Cleon, who we know gathered support from the poor and the old through measures like his increase in jury-pay? Plutarch (*Nicias* 2.3) quotes an unknown comic poet (Adespota fr. 740 *PCG*) who describes Cleon 'coddling old men and giving out jobs for pay' and relates (*Moralia* 806f-807a) that when Cleon decided to enter politics, he broke off his friendships and allied himself with 'worst and most corrupt elements of the demos' against the aristocrats (cf. *Cavalry* 255–7, 852–4 for Cleon's supporters). When Paphlagon in *Cavalry* accuses Agorakritos of thinking he could make a good speech because he had defeated a metic in a trifling case (347–50), could it be that Cleon understood how metics and freed slaves suffered in Athens' judicial system through nothing other than their lack of Athenian citizenship? Was Cleon in fact known as a defender of marginalized groups in Athens, whether through cynical political calculus or even genuine altruism? As we remarked earlier, it is extremely hard to discern the man behind the mask of Paphlagon.

Reconstructing a balanced view of Cleon is an impossible task due to the bias inherent in the remaining sources. But it is at least possible to complicate the picture of Cleon as a disastrous politician, a cowardly commander and a comic villain that has been painted for us, above all, by his contemporaries Thucydides and Aristophanes and accepted by later writers, ancient and modern. Doing this is important for reaching a fuller understanding of the historical background to *Cavalry* and some of the subtle ways, pointed out in the following chapters, in which the Sausage-Seller Agorakritos is characterized as a leader even worse than Paphlagon.

3

Cavalry 1–302: Prologue and Parodos

The first sequence of stage action in *Cavalry* (1–302) contains the 'prologue' and the 'parodos' (the term for the 'entrance of the chorus'). It introduces the 'backstory' and all the characters, except the old man Demos. Many of the play's themes, images, metaphors and motifs are present. All relate to the corrupt nature of politics and politicians in Athens dominated by the demagogue Cleon. The central metaphor is the enslavement of the leaders of Athens to the people – an expression of extreme populism and one of the many images found in the play of inverted political and social relationships and practices. In this sequence, the audience also encounters the themes of the debased character of Athens' leaders (shamelessness and outrageous behaviour), their dangerous rhetoric (especially flattery of the people) and its consequences (political chaos and confusion).

Prologue (1–246)

In Aristophanes, a prologue begins either with a monologue delivered by an important character, or a dialogue, which may involve central or marginal characters. In *Cavalry*, the prologue begins with a dialogue between two slaves. It establishes the 'backstory' and sets a trajectory for the narrative arc of the play. As in all Aristophanes' surviving plays, plot and action are motivated by a political or social crisis in the city of Athens. In response, a heroic (or anti-heroic) character will take on the task of resolving or escaping the crisis; he (or less frequently she) may act on altruistic or egocentric motives and will usually employ improbable or fantastical means. An eventual triumph of some kind is assured, but it may not be all that the heroic character originally intended or what the audience has been led to expect.

The crisis in *Acharnians*, *Peace* and *Lysistrata* is how to make peace with Sparta, whether individually or collectively; in *Clouds*, the dangers of sophistic education; in *Wasps*, corruption in the courts; in *Women at the Thesmophoria*, the social effects of Euripides' tragedies; in *Frogs*, the decline of tragic drama; and in *Assembly Women* and *Wealth*, widespread poverty. In *Cavalry* the problem is the power of the demagogue Cleon and his corrupting influence on Athenian democracy.

Almost every surviving Aristophanic comedy begins with the expression of some negative emotion: boredom, anger, frustration, anxiety, and so on. *Cavalry* begins with an inarticulate howl of pain as a slave emerges from a house after a beating. The house, as the audience soon discovers, belongs to an old man called Demos – a personification of the Athenian citizenry, whose name means 'the people' (Gk. *dēmos*). The slave curses another slave called Paphlagon, who, though only recently purchased, has become their master's favourite and taken control of the household. Such is Paphlagon's influence, he can even arrange to have his fellow slaves whipped by their master (1–5).

Paphlagon is a cipher for Cleon, Athens' leading demagogue in the mid-420s BCE: abundant evidence in *Cavalry* makes this clear, as does an intertextual passage in *Clouds* (581–6). The name Paphlagon identifies this character as a slave from Paphlagonia, a region in northern Asia Minor on the Black Sea: foreign slaves in Athens were often given an 'ethnic' name, designating their place of origin. Accusations levelled at prominent citizens of foreign or slave ancestry are a staple of the humour of Aristophanes and other poets of Old Comedy and a real feature of political oratory.[1] The allegorical representation of Cleon as a slave of Demos is the play's 'central metaphor' (Newiger 1957: esp. 14–15): the leaders of Athens have become slaves of the people and therefore behave like slaves: obsequious, thieving and deceitful, they have turned Athenian politics and society upside down and thrown the city into chaos.

There are further reasons for Aristophanes' choice of the name 'Paphlagon'. It sounds like and is derived from (cf. Eupolis fr. 192.135-6

Storey) the Greek word *paphlazein*, meaning to 'bubble' or 'seethe' like boiling water (e.g. *Cavalry* 919) or rough seas (e.g. Homer, *Iliad* 13.798; *Cavalry* 431–2); used metaphorically of speech, it means to 'splutter' or 'speak bombastically'. In this way, Paphlagon's name suits his style of speech and the turbulent political effects of his rhetoric. Aristophanes repeatedly attacks Cleon for his horrible, loud voice (e.g. 137, 275, 287, 304, 311 etc.; cf. *Wasps* 36) and for the political upheaval that he causes in the city.[2]

The slave who screams in pain will soon be identified, through a reference to the recent military campaign at Pylos (see Chapter 2), as the Athenian general Demosthenes (54–7). This Demosthenes is not to be confused with Demosthenes the famous fourth-century politician and rhetorician. The second slave, who accompanies Demosthenes out of the house, may be identified as the general Nicias; this is suggested by his unwillingness to fight (14), his fearfulness and caution (17), his religiosity (30–4) and his aversion to wine (87–9, 97; cf. Sommerstein 1980: 46–7; Sommerstein 1981: 3; MacDowell 1995: 87–8; Wilson 2007b: 39). The historical Demosthenes and Nicias had both been involved in the action at Pylos that ended with Cleon's triumphant capture of 292 Peloponnesian soldiers: Demosthenes had served at Pylos as the Cleon's colleague in command, and Nicias had relinquished his command to Cleon, thereby seeming to avoid fighting the campaign himself (cf. Thucydides 3.27-9).[3]

The identification of the two slaves as Demosthenes and Nicias has sometimes been questioned by modern scholars because in the manuscripts of *Cavalry* their lines are marked only by the notations 'First Slave' and 'Second Slave'. However, the ancient copyists and editors of *Cavalry* (known as 'scholiasts') made the identification of Demosthenes in their notes (known as 'scholia', designated by the Greek letter Σ), and both Demosthenes and Nicias are named in an ancient introduction to the play and a cast-list. In this book, the names Demosthenes and Nicias are adopted for several reasons. First, the characterization of the two slaves mentioned above fits well with what we know about the historical Demosthenes and Nicias. Second, the identification was made in antiquity by the scholiasts. Third, Cleon, Demosthenes and Nicias were the three Athenian commanders most heavily involved in the military action at Pylos the year before the production of *Cavalry,* and Pylos and its political ramifications are a central theme of the play.[4]

Nicias joins Demosthenes and the two slaves express their shared misery. Such is their distress that they cry, their sobs imitating the sound of flutes, and the notes of their dirge (Gk. *mumū,* repeated six times) occupying a full line of the play (10). It is very unusual for Aristophanes to write an entire verse of inarticulate sounds outside lyric passages. The striking form of this line heavily emphasizes Demosthenes and Nicias' wretchedness, as does Demosthenes' question (11) 'Why are we doing nothing but wail?' The word for 'wail' used by Demosthenes, (Gk.) *kinuresthai,* is rare and elevated in tone (prior to *Cavalry* it is only found in Aeschylus); again, it emphasizes their despair.[5] The slaves' inarticulacy – their fearful avoidance of speech – in this sequence is the beginning of a thematic progression (Hubbard 1991: 65; Littlefield 1968: 6–7). To confront Paphlagon will require a man with words so audacious that they will silence Athens' most violent and persuasive speaker. Neither of the two generals is up to the task that will soon fall to a humble 'sausage-seller'.[6]

Demosthenes follows his first question with another (11–12): 'Shouldn't the two of us stop crying and search for some way of escape for ourselves?' The Greek word translated here by 'way of escape' is *sōtēria* ('safety', 'salvation', or 'escape') – it is an Aristophanic trope. Aristophanes frequently designs comic plots as the hero's quest for *sōtēria,* whether for the city or the hero alone (e.g. *Clouds* 77, *Peace* 301, *Lysistrata* 30, *Women at the Thesmophoria* 186, *Frogs* 1436). In *Cavalry,* in addition to Demosthenes and Nicias' longing for 'escape' from their woes, the sausage-seller, the character who saves Athens, is twice hailed with the related word 'saviour' (Gk. *sōtēr*): he is called 'saviour of the city' (149) and 'saviour of the city and its citizens' (458). By contrast, whenever Paphlagon speaks of 'safety', he only wants it for himself, not for the city or its citizens (1017, 1024, 1042).[7]

In the next sequence, the two slaves discuss how to find safety in the current crisis. But the discussion is impeded by Nicias' characteristic timidity: he is hesitant to say what he has in mind and attempts to manoeuvre Demosthenes into speaking first (17–18, 16), quoting a well-known line of Euripides' play *Hippolytus* (428 BCE). The verse, 'How might you say for me what I need to say?' (*Hippolytus* 345), is drawn from the scene in which Phaedra, who has fallen in love with her stepson Hippolytus, manipulates her nurse into pronouncing Hippolytus' name and so revealing the disastrous passion that has gripped her mistress. Once more, inarticulacy defines the opening of the play, suggesting the apparent impossibility of doing anything about Paphlagon. The quotation of Aristophanes' favourite tragedian is followed by a joke at Euripides' expense. Demosthenes rebukes Nicias (19) with the words 'You won't get *parsley* me like that!': the mention of 'parsley' alludes to the humorous, but doubtless untrue, allegation that Euripides' mother had been a vegetable-seller, one of Aristophanes' favourite jokes repeated in his comedies over many years (*Acharnians* 478; *Women at the Thesmophoria* 387; *Frogs* 840).[8]

Nicias tries again. This time he succeeds in making Demosthenes suggest that they flee the house by telling him to repeat the phrases 'away lets' and 'run', gradually faster and faster, as though he were masturbating, until he exclaims 'let's run away!' (21–6). Demosthenes remarks that Nicias' plan is 'ill-omened', joking that masturbation has something in common with being flogged (a typical punishment for slaves) – in each case skin peels back (27–9).

Nicias reconsiders: they should claim sanctuary ('supplication': see Chapter 7) by falling at the feet of one of the statues of the gods (30–1), only for Demosthenes to ridicule his timidity by pretending to stammer 'What st-st-statue?' (32).[9] A typical Aristophanic plot sequence is developed here. Aristophanes' prologues often see one or more simple solutions to the opening crisis proposed, before a character hits on the improbable or fantastical plan that the plot will follow (Kloss 2001: 252–61). This sequence in *Cavalry* is particularly extensive: three solutions thought up by Nicias (running away, taking sanctuary and committing suicide) are rejected before Demosthenes, inspired by wine, finds the answer in an oracle. The unusually long search for a plan in *Cavalry* highlights the extreme challenge that Paphlagon presents.

At this point, Demosthenes suggests that he explain the situation to the audience (36). Nicias agrees and asks the audience to show them with their faces if they are enjoying the performance so far (37–9). Breaches of the theatrical illusion are very common in Old Comedy. A remark about or an address to the audience occurs most often in the parabasis (in *Cavalry*, see 546–7), where it is conventional, but references to 'the spectators' of the play frequently appear elsewhere (in *Cavalry*, see 228, 1210). The extent to which an Athenian audience participated when invited to is unknown but given the evidence for audience behaviour when they disliked a production, it is not unlikely that they would respond positively as well.[10]

Demosthenes' speech explains the scenario (40–72). First, he tells the audience about his master, 'Demos of the Pnyx' (42), whose household is dominated by a slave called Paphlagon who is a tanner (44). Though 'Demos' is attested as a personal name in classical Athens (*LGPN* p. 110), here it has a clear allegorical meaning: the slaves' master personifies the Athenian citizenry – more specifically the citizens of Athens *in the democratic assembly*, since the Pnyx, a low hill west of the acropolis, was the assembly's usual meeting place (for a map, see Figure 1). For all the criticism directed at Demos in the play, Aristophanes is careful to emphasize that the assembly, not the people themselves, is the problem (cf. 752–5). The identity of the slave-tanner Paphlagon will have been easy to guess for the audience, since it was well-known that Cleon owned a tannery: in *Acharnians* (299–301), performed the previous year, the phrase 'Cleon whom I'm going to cut up into shoe-leather' would only have comic potential if the audience was familiar with Cleon's family business. The game being played with the audience here – interpreting metaphors and allusions – is a convention in comic prologues: in *Peace* (43–8) Aristophanes makes a metatheatrical joke about audiences expecting prologues to contain interpretive puzzles.

The function of slavery in the allegory of Demos' household deserves further comment. At one level, it is an extended version of a favourite Aristophanic joke: that is, prominent politicians were not in fact Athenian citizens because they were slaves or the descendants of slaves. At a deeper level, the allegory suggests that the proper relationship between the assembly and its elected leaders (like the annually elected generals) has been corrupted. Whereas leaders should lead by persuading the assembly to vote in the general interest of the polis, Cleon and his ilk now serve the ephemeral wants and needs of the assembly and neglect genuine leadership of Athens. Moreover, since Demos has become dependent on his slave politicians for state-pay and other favours, Paphlagon has taken over Demos' house and turned the master to some extent into his slave (cf. Olson 2013: esp. 69–72).

The dynamics in *Cavalry* of the corrupt relationship between politicians and people are expressed in two main ways. First, politicians have become 'flatterers' (Gk. *kolakes*) of the people instead of leaders, mirroring the relationship between a rich dupe and his dissembling parasites, who would flatter, entertain and perform menial service for him in return for hospitality (cf. Tylawsky 2002: esp. 19–23); such adulation implicitly figures the people as a tyrant, the greatest target of flatterers, and politicians as his self-abasing subjects (cf. *Cavalry* 1111–20; Edwards 2010: 322–30). Second, the play presents politicians as pederastic lovers of Demos but reframes the idealized, altruistic Greek homoerotic relationship of mature lover and mentor (Gk. *erastēs*) and his beloved youth (Gk. *erōmenos*) as the mutually exploitative transactional arrangements of prostitute and client (Wohl 2002: 73–123).

Having introduced Paphlagon, Demosthenes recounts a list of the strategies he uses to win over Demos (46–52). He begins with Paphlagon's obsequiousness. This tactic is presented as paramount: it appears first and is emphasized with a tricolon, a rhetorical device employing a sequence of three juxtaposed expressions without syntactical connection. All are words for flattery, one of the play's thematic images: 'he began *fawning, flattering, sucking up* ...' (48).[11] And so, Demosthenes continues (50–2), Paphlagon deceived Demos with scraps of leather, offering the old man a bath, serving up food and doling out jury-pay (the 'three obols': Gk. *triōbolon*). The last of these is strongly associated with Cleon because he had increased pay for jurors from two to three obols a day (see further, Markle 1985: 1 n. 1). This policy had apparently proved very popular with elderly Athenians who were unlikely to find other income. In consequence, many jurors had become supporters of Cleon, a phenomenon memorably satirized by Aristophanes in *Wasps*; but it appears in *Cavalry* too: for example, when Paphlagon is attacked by the chorus, he calls for help from the 'brotherhood of the three obols' (255, cf. 800).

Paphlagon's use of food to curry favour with Demos (51–2) is only the first instance of an important theme in *Cavalry*: food as a political metaphor (Hubbard 1991: 68–9; Whitman 1964: 92–6; Wilkins 2000: 187–92). This is highlighted in the play's first reference to Cleon's victory at Pylos (54–7) which is figured as a barley-cake, appropriately enough since Cleon was rewarded with free meals in the Prytaneion. Similarly, the hostages from Pylos are frequently presented as food (e.g. 391–4, 742–5, 1053, 1167), as are many forms of political success, persuasion and corruption throughout the play. For example, food represents the means, like jury-pay, by which demagogues win the favour of the Demos (e.g. 51–2, 60, 215–16), and extravagant consumption represents political corruption (e.g. 359–60). The power of food is seen in Paphlagon's tactic of preventing other politicians from feeding Demos (58–60).

Next, Demosthenes says that Paphlagon recites oracles to Demos, who is thoroughly taken in: the old man has gone 'Sibyl-crazy' (61). The Sibyl was an inspired prophetess whose name was a metonym for divination. Divination will emerge as a central theme in *Cavalry*: not only does Paphlagon use prophecies to enhance his power over Demos, but his fall is predicted and confirmed by an oracle (see below and Chapters 6 and 8).

Lastly, Demosthenes explains how Paphlagon keeps control of the other slaves in the household. He has them whipped by Demos by making false accusations, and he threatens and extorts them (63–70). The implications of Demosthenes' words are that Cleon uses political slanders and prosecutions to intimidate and remove his enemies and to exact bribes. If Aristophanes was in fact prosecuted by Cleon (see Chapter 2), he will have had firsthand experience of such tactics. Malicious prosecutions, slander, threats and extortion are the hallmarks of Paphlagon's techniques for dealing with his enemies; they will figure repeatedly in the play until the demagogue is defeated. Here, there is even a hint of assassination (68), a relatively rare occurrence in Athenian political life (Bearzot 2007).

Demosthenes ends his speech by returning to the urgent question of what he and Nicias should do (71–2). Nicias suggests again that they run away. But nothing escapes Paphlagon's notice: in a striking image of monstrosity, Demosthenes imagines Paphlagon as a colossus bestriding Attica and the Peloponnese, with one leg in Pylos, the other in the assembly in Athens, and his anus, with an obscene pun, 'in a gaping chasm'; the latter is only the first example of the motif of the successful politician as pathic, i.e. a man who plays the role of the passive partner in homosexual sex (see esp. *Cavalry* 423–6; Henderson 1991: 68). Aristophanes repeatedly figures Cleon as a monster (*Wasps* 1029–35, *Peace* 752–8).

Nicias decides that the best thing is for them to die (80) and suggests drinking bull's blood, as Themistocles, a leading politician of the period of the Persian Wars (cf. 813–16), was popularly believed to have done (83–4; cf. Plutarch, *Themistocles* 31.5-6; Marr 1995).[12] The adaptation of some verses of Sophocles ('Better for me to drink bull's blood and endure their slanders no longer' = fr. 178 Lloyd-Jones) gives Nicias' words a suitably tragic ring (83). Demosthenes is unconvinced, but the mention of drinking gives him an idea: getting drunk will inspire him to come up with a plan (85–6). Nicias is sent back into the house, where he steals some wine, while Paphlagon is snoring in a drunken stupor, flat on his back on a pile of hides (101–4).

Once Nicias brings out the wine, Demosthenes holds his own 'symposium', a ritualized drinking party that was a prominent feature of ancient Greek culture. In a number of ways, Demosthenes breaks the conventions of the symposium. He is the only guest at the party, and he drinks the wine neat (85), shockingly contrary to the usual Greek practice, which was to mix wine with water (cf. 354–5). Traditionally the symposium began with a taste of unmixed wine and a libation of it poured to the 'Good Spirit' (Gk. *agathos daimōn*). By custom, this was the only time Greeks drank undiluted wine, and the name of Zeus the Saviour was intoned over the cup, apparently as a reminder that wine must be mixed with water to be safe. Against Nicias' advice, Demosthenes drinks the libation himself (106–8) and carries on drinking neat wine, ignoring Nicias' objections and concerns (87–8, 97, 111–12, 124).[13] The unusual conduct of Demosthenes' symposium is one of the play's many images of the corruption and inversion of institutions and practices.

Inebriation quickly inspires Demosthenes, and he tells Nicias to go back into the house and steal Paphlagon's oracles (109–11). Nicias returns with Paphlagon's 'sacred oracle' (116, cf. 152–3, 194), which foretells how he will be ousted from power. The oracle comes from Apollo's shrine at Delphi (220; cf. 1229), indicating its unquestionable authority and contrasting it with the many prophecies found later in the play (see Chapter 6).

Demosthenes reads Paphlagon's oracle, discovering that it predicts a (quasi-mythical: see Bowie 1993: 58–66) succession of leaders of the demos, all involved in trades (128–44). Ancient Greek aristocrats liked to present themselves as men whose wealth came from land, not from commerce, manufacturing, or markets; they generally regarded those who made money in such ways as dishonest (Demosthenes 36.44) and frequently used their business to disparage them: for example, Aeschines (2.93) insults the fourth-century politician Demosthenes as the 'son of a knife-maker' (for further examples, see Dover 1974: 30–3).

Demosthenes' perusal of the oracle reveals that the last demagogue but one (i.e. Paphlagon) will be a leather-seller with a hideous voice, but he is finally to be defeated by a man of even more unusual profession: a sausage-seller (143–4). These revelations predict how the plot will unfold up to Paphlagon's final defeat (1253). No sooner are the oracle's secrets known, than a sausage-seller miraculously appears, on his way to the market (146–7); he probably enters stage right, since in the

Theatre of Dionysus he would then be heading westwards, in the direction of the Athens' marketplace (Gk. *agorā*). For the sake of simplicity, this character will be referred to throughout as Agorakritos, but it is important to remember that the audience does not find out the sausage-seller's name until much later in the play (1257). Demosthenes encourages this new character to come up out of the *orkhēstra* and on to the stage (149).[14]

Immediately after Agorakritos arrives, Nicias returns to the house to keep watch over Paphlagon (154), for the actor playing Nicias probably also plays the role of Paphlagon; if so, *Cavalry* was performed, like a tragedy, with only three speaking actors.[15] This structural feature of the performance emphasizes the paratragic nature of Paphlagon's fall (Chapter 8), when the truth of the Delphic oracle is confirmed – a plot device familiar from tragedy, notably in Sophocles' *Oedipus Tyrannus*, which was probably produced not long before *Cavalry* and perhaps shaped its plot-construction.[16] In this respect, *Cavalry* is unique among Aristophanes' surviving plays: no other play dramatizes the fall of a 'paratragic villain', whose doom is also the comic hero's success. It is also Aristophanes' only surviving play without any speaking female roles; the focus is decidedly on the public, male world of Athenian politics.

Demosthenes encourages Agorakritos to put down his worktable (152) and other tools of his trade (155) and to prostrate himself on the ground in worship of Earth and the gods (155–6). He does as he is told (157). It is notable that, though Agorakritos is fully prepared to swear a false oath (297–8; cf. 418–28, 1239), as is Paphlagon (299), his action here (repeated at 640) shows more piety than Paphlagon ever does. The latter's only religious act is a ridiculous (and therefore insincere) prayer to Athene (763–4). But elsewhere, Agorakritos shows himself, in all sorts of ways, to be worse than Paphlagon, just as the oracle requires (and is necessary for the element of surprise in the play's ending).

Demosthenes hails Agorakritos in exaggerated terms (157–9), leading him to think that he is being ridiculed (161), as indeed he is. Next, he calls him an 'idiot' (162) and foretells his rise to become the leader of Athens, saying with a glance at the audience (164–7):

Demosthenes   Of all these men you shall be the grandmaster,
And of the marketplace, the docks, and the Pnyx.
You'll walk all over the Council, you'll prune the generals,
Shackle, imprison, and in the Prytaneion you'll eat dick!

The joke in the last line exemplifies a very common technique of Aristophanic humour – the figure of speech known as the 'paraprosdokian', in which the last element of a sequence of words comes as a surprise replacement of something more obvious. Here, the expectation created by the words 'in the Prytaneion you'll . . .' is that the sentence will end with 'eat dinner'. The sexual joke at Agorakritos' expense is also a frequent feature of Aristophanes' humour: politicians in Aristophanes are almost universally assumed to be prostitutes and pathics, for this is how political success is achieved (Aristophanes makes a version of this joke in Plato's *Symposium* 192a). Notably, Agorakritos takes no offence at Demosthenes' words: later it will transpire that he has in fact prostituted himself (1241–2).

Demosthenes directs Agorakritos to perform an eye-catching piece of stage action. He tells Agorakritos to climb on to his table and view the Athenian empire (169–74), for he will soon rule over it all. Symbolically, this action prefigures Agorakritos' ascent from the dregs of society to the leadership of Athens (Hubbard 1991: 67). Agorakritos stands on the table he has brought with him (cf. 152) and turns around in a circle (170). Demosthenes tells him to cast his gaze rightwards to Caria and left toward Carthage. Since an actor facing the audience in the Theatre of Dionysus faces north, Demosthenes' directions are geographically accurate (173–4). This suggests that Agorakritos turns clockwise from north, since after looking toward the islands of the Aegean (from north-east to south-west), he confirms (171–2) that he can see the trading port and merchant ships: this would suggest that at this point he is facing Piraeus, roughly to the west of the theatre (for a map, see Figure 1).

Agorakritos' turn will have allowed the audience a full view of his mask and costume from every angle: it is possible that his padded comic costume was unusually hideous and bulging, for he later describes using his backside as a battering ram (640–1). Actors in Old Comedy (see the vase in Figure 2) were costumed in loose 'tights' and a padded torso (Gk. *sōmation*) with protuberant breasts, stomach and buttocks, and a large dangling phallus. The mask (Gk. *prosōpon*), shown above and to the left of the central figure on the vase, was an elaborate three-quarter construction, covering the actor's whole head, with exaggerated (and usually ugly) features.[17]

Demosthenes tells Agorakritos about the oracle, probably a papyrus scroll, which he is holding (177), and which predicts that a sausage-seller will become a 'great man' (178: Gk. *anēr megistos*). Agorakritos asks how a sausage-seller can could ever become a man at all. The joke in Greek here (cf. 333, 1255) relies on the fact that the word for 'a man' (*anēr*) can mean both someone who is simply an adult male or someone who is a 'real man': that is, one who displays ideal masculine qualities and is a respected public figure. It is notable that when Agorakritos triumphs over Paphlagon, Demosthenes reappears briefly to remind him that he has become 'a man' because of him (1254–5), and that Paphlagon calls himself a 'man' more than once (765, 790): the evolution of the plot is marked by Agorakritos' journey from no man at all to the greatest one in Athens.[18]

To become not just 'a man' but a 'great man' would normally imply aristocratic birth, wealth, education and notable contributions to public life. The standard term for 'the aristocracy' in ancient Greek was *hoi kaloi k'agathoi* (literally, 'the noble and good'); it is used in the play to refer to the traditional leaders of the people (cf. 227, 735, 738), as is the term *khrēstos* ('decent' or 'of worth', 192). But in the world of *Cavalry*, being a 'great man' means *not* being from an aristocratic family but from the lowest or poorest (Gk. *ponēros*) background (185–7).[19] Whereas leadership of the people once belonged to men who had learned music, the highest level of education (cf. 188, 191), now a man suited to politics is one, like Agorakritos, who has as little education as possible, and certainly none in music (188–90); note that failure in musical education is something that will later be attributed to Cleon in the only passage in the play that refers to him directly (985–96). In short, when it comes to the leadership of Athens, traditional aristocratic politicians are out and the lowest of the low are in (191–3), another of the images of social inversion in Paphlagon's Athens.

Heartened by Demosthenes' encouragement, Agorakritos asks what the oracle says (195). Demosthenes reads out five verses of the oracle (197–201):

> 'Yet when the crooked-clawed leathern eagle snatches up
> The stupid blood-gorged snake in its beak –
> In that moment the pickled garlic of the Paphlagons is vanquished,
> And the god bestows great splendour upon the Sausage Sellers,
> If they choose not to sell sausages instead.'

Ancient Greek oracles were composed in hexameter verses (the meter of the epic poetry, like that of Hesiod and Homer), and in elevated, archaic and enigmatic language (cf. 196). Humour is generated here by vocabulary inappropriate in an oracular text, like 'stupid', 'pickled garlic' and 'sausages'. The oracle's imagery and, therefore, its symbolic meaning will have been familiar to the original audience. The model is taken from the *Iliad* (12.200–7), where an eagle seizes a snake but is bitten by it, indicating that in conflict the apparently losing adversary will deny his opponent victory; indeed, this is how the omen is interpreted in Homer (ibid. 210–29). The image of the eagle and the snake is also found in *Wasps* (15–19) and on a gravestone of an Athenian seer from the first half of the fourth century (*SEG* 16.193).

Demosthenes explains the oracle, indicating with a gesture that the 'leathern eagle' is 'this Paphlagon here' (203), pointing to Cleon, who will have been seated in the front-row of the audience in honour of his victory at Pylos.[20] The serpent, he continues, is a sausage (207–10), indicating that Agorakritos has been chosen to overcome the leather eagle. Agorakritos replies (211–12) that although he is flattered by the oracle – one of the intended effects of oracles used in political rhetoric, as events later in the play will make clear (Chapter 6) – he doubts that he has the ability to lead the people. Demosthenes replies that

Agorakritos is eminently suited to the task, describing the qualities now needed for a man to succeed in Athens. He introduces the theme of 'stirring up' chaos and confusion (Gk. *tarattein*: generally, 'to stir up' or 'confound'; see Chapter 5), advising Agorakritos to mix up politics just as he hashes up the ingredients of his sausages and to sweeten the people by applying his culinary skills to words (214–16) – another example of the motif of food as a symbol of political success (and perhaps the faintest of hints about the importance of cookery at the end of the play). Agorakritos, Demosthenes continues, already has the other qualities of a 'demagogue': a horrible voice, low birth, and making a living as a market trader (217–18).

Agorakritos doubts that he can defeat Paphlagon without support. Here, Demosthenes announces that help will come from various quarters. First, the cavalry, who form the chorus of the play, will come to Agorakritos' aid. The chorus is introduced (225) in terms that make them the social antithesis of demagogues: they are nobly born aristocrats (Gk. *agathoi*). Next, all the elite in the city (227) and anyone in the audience who is smart (228) will help, as will Demosthenes and even 'the god', meaning Apollo, from whom the oracle comes (229, cf. 220). Lastly, Demosthenes reassures Agorakritos that he will not have to fear Paphlagon's face because the mask-makers were too frightened to make an accurate representation (230–2) – probably a joke meaning that Cleon's appearance is even more hideous than the ugly masks used in Greek comedy.[21]

Nicias' voice is heard from within the house warning them that Paphlagon is about to emerge (234). On his first appearance, Paphlagon employs some his characteristic tactics: accusations and threats. He claims the wine cup Demosthenes has been using (237, cf. 95–102) is from the city of Chalcis on the island of Euboea and he accuses Demosthenes and Agorakritos of fomenting a rebellion there (236, 238–9).[22] The allegation of plotting is one that Paphlagon often uses (cf. 257, 452, 476–7, 628, 862). It was a serious charge: betraying the city or subverting the democracy were among the few offences carrying mandatory imprisonment (cf. Demosthenes 24.144).

Agorakritos starts to run off the stage in terror (240), so Demosthenes summons the chorus to come to the rescue (242). He calls out to two men in particular, Simon and Panaitios, who may have been real-life cavalry commanders.[23] Demosthenes gives orders in military fashion (as the scholiasts note: Σ 243), such as 'won't you drive towards the right wing?' (243). Such words are fitting for the historical Demosthenes, who was an experienced general. He encourages Agorakritos to turn and face Paphlagon (243, 246), which suggests that between verses 240 and 243 Agorakritos must have run some distance – probably across the *orkhēstra*, for the actors used that space as well as the raised stage as a playing area. From line 242, Demosthenes' words change their rhythm from the ordinary meter of 'speech' (iambic trimeters) to a chanted meter suited to the parodos (the entrance of the chorus). This and the dust cloud imagined to be rising offstage (245) prepare the audience for the appearance of the cavalry.

Parodos (247–302)

The chorus of Athenian cavalry enter the *orkhēstra*, chanting their first lines (247–54) in trochaic tetrameters, a meter that conveys heightened emotion, in this case the excitement of battle. The comic chorus of 24 dancers was central to productions of Old Comedy. When a comic poet had a play in mind, it was for 'a chorus' that he asked the archon. In a sense, the chorus was synonymous with the production, and it certainly contributed centrally to its success or failure (e.g. *Clouds* 1115–16, where the judges are asked to 'help *this chorus*').

There is a lot of uncertainty about the costume of *Cavalry*'s chorus. A black-figure amphora (dating to about a hundred years before the performance of *Cavalry*) depicts a chorus of riders mounted piggyback on other members of the chorus who are dressed in horse costumes (Figure 3); it has been offered as evidence that the chorus of *Cavalry* could have been mounted on some representation of horses. This might have meant a chorus costumed half as riders and half as horses with the riders carried by the horses at some point in the action, or perhaps a chorus riding some kind of 'hobby horses'. Alternatively, it is possible that the chorus were not costumed as horses at all but merely danced in a way understood to represent horse-riders.

The chorus joins Demosthenes in encouraging Agorakritos to get to grips with Paphlagon, to fight him and to shout out loud. They probably dance around Paphlagon, hitting him (247, 251, cf. 257, 266, 273), driving him about (251) and encircling him to stop him from getting away (253). It is worth noting that while Agorakritos and his allies descend to physical violence (cf. 451–6), Paphlagon does not, one of the subtler ways in which characterization shows Agorakritos up as even worse than his opponent. The chorus accuse Paphlagon of extortion and theft (248) and of throwing the cavalry into confusion (247), another image of political commotion and chaos. Since this is the first encounter in the play between Paphlagon and the cavalry, the reference should be to some extra-dramatic event – perhaps Cleon's cancelling or reducing public funding for the cavalry corps (see Chapter 2).

Paphlagon calls for help from the old jurymen who are 'brothers of the order of the three obols' (evoking Cleon's increase of jury-pay from two obols to three), appealing to them to defend him against the 'conspirators' who are beating him up (255). It is possible that Paphlagon's attempt to summon 'the old men of the courts' hints that Aristophanes had already conceived the idea of writing the play that in two years' time would become *Wasps*. But primarily it is a metatheatrical joke: the chorus is already on stage, so Paphlagon's attempt to summon another one will be fruitless.

In reply, the chorus accuses Paphlagon of embezzlement (258) and 'sycophancy' (259–60). A literal translation of the term sycophancy is 'revealing figs', apparently deriving from an ancient law of Solon against the export of figs from Attica, but its etymology is obscure; by the fifth century a sycophant meant a man who threatened or made a frivolous prosecution (for a comic depiction of such a character, see *Wealth* 850–950) – one that had no merit and from which the accuser stood to benefit.[24] In Greek Old Comedy, many mentions of figs or fig trees contain a joke about corrupt litigiousness (e.g. *Wasps* 897; *Birds* 1699). This is the case here, where Paphlagon is accused of auditing magistrates at the end of their term of office by squeezing them like figs to find the ripe ones. The theme of corruption continues with the allegation that Paphlagon prosecutes rich men who want nothing to do with politics – by implication making money from the case (261–5).

Disappointed of any help from his allies, Paphlagon attempts to win over the chorus with the promise of an assembly motion to erect a memorial to the cavalry's bravery on the acropolis (266–8; possibly a reference to the battle of Solygeia: see Chapter 4), but the chorus is unimpressed by his attempt at flattery (269–70). They perform a manoeuvre, probably to block Paphlagon (271–2). The use of flattering rhetoric and empty promises (to win over the demos) will become a prominent theme later in the play, especially in the second agon (303–460; see Chapter 5).

The final section of the parodos sees Agorakritos, who has been silent so far, overcome his inarticulacy and summon the courage to face Paphlagon. Agorakritos' first words (274) accuse Paphlagon of turning the city upside-down, another of many images of social inversion found in the play. The chorus characterize the rivalry between Agorakritos and Paphlagon as a competition in 'outrageousness' (277: Gk. *anaideia*), an important motif in next sequence of the play (see Chapter 4).

From this point, the ordinary structure of the parodos begins to break down. Usually, the chorus dominates the whole sequence, but here they are interrupted as Paphlagon and Agorakritos become the focus of the stage action, each accusing the other of theft of public resources (275–83). Agorakritos and Demosthenes' accusations, that Paphlagon has exploited his recently won dining rights, develop the theme of food representing political power (280–3): even Pericles, Demosthenes says, a leader respected far more than Cleon, never deserved the kind of meals at public expense that Paphlagon enjoys (282–3).

The parodos closes with a run of short verses, known as a 'pnigos', literally a 'choker'; it is found in various poetic structures in Old Comedy. The reason for its name (cf. Σ *Acharnians* 659) is that in it one or more runs of short lines were pronounced in a single breath – a demonstration of the actor's skill (see *Clouds* 1009–23 for an extended example). In many cases, however, the lines of a pnigos are divided between two actors, and the short verses simply increase the tempo of delivery and emotional intensity. Here, the pnigos (284–304) sees Paphlagon and Agorakritos trade insulting and inventive threats with great rapidity. The division of most of their dialogue (284–96) into alternating single lines ('stichomythia') is unusual in a pnigos: the effect is one of virtuoso, rapid-fire 'trash-talking', as the two main characters of *Cavalry* square up to one another for the first time. Each aims to outdo the other in a poetic 'capping competition', a feature found in many places in the play (e.g. 351–81, 441–81; see Hesk 2007: esp. 141–50).

The marginalization of the chorus and the fragmentation of the traditional structure of the parodos makes a metatheatrical point, as the end of the parodos begins to do the work of the next formal sequence, the 'agon' (or 'contest'), even before it begins (Gelzer 1960: 12). The chorus attempt to maintain their traditional role, fitting their character as traditionalist aristocrats, but Paphlagon and Agorakritos disrupt formal sequences of action (here and elsewhere): the subversion of dramatic conventions symbolizes the chaos and confusion in Athenian political life that demagogues cause.

4

Cavalry 303–610: First Agon and Parabasis

The second sequence of *Cavalry* contains an agon (the Greek word for 'contest') and, after a short linking episode, a parabasis (a choral address to the audience). The agon is a struggle between Paphlagon and Agorakritos over who can demonstrate the greatest 'outrageousness'. The result is a furious exchange of boasts, threats, oaths, accusations and insults. As at every stage of the plot, Agorakritos finds a way to outdo his adversary.

During the parabasis, Paphlagon and Agorakritos are offstage competing for the favour of the council. The chorus address the audience on behalf of Aristophanes, explaining why *Cavalry* is the first play that he has directed himself, rather than writing the script for another comic director: salutary tales of the (alleged) failures of other comic poets dissuaded him from competing as a director before he was ready. In the second part of the parabasis, the chorus pray to Athene and Poseidon and praise the military exploits of their ancestors and of Nicias in a recent campaign against Corinth. The selfless martial valour of the Athenians' forebears and of Nicias contrasts with Cleon's self-aggrandizing triumph at Pylos.

Agon (303–460)

Aristophanes uses the dramatic sequence known as the 'agon' (Gk. *agōn*) in many of his plays. It is a formal element of Greek drama found in tragedy, satyr-play and comedy. Aristophanes makes its importance and conventional nature clear in numerous metatheatrical references (e.g. *Acharnians* 481, *Clouds* 957, *Wasps* 533, *Frogs* 882). In its traditional form, the agon is a debate between two speakers over a central issue in the play.

The poetic design of the agon is a structure known as an 'epirrhematic syzygy' (i.e. 'a double structure of speeches'): an A-B-A-B sequence of song-speech-song-speech. The chorus introduces the speakers in turn with a short ode before each makes a long speech or a series of speeches. The two odes are called the 'strophe' and the 'antistrophe', indicating that they are composed in 'strophic responsion', meaning that the metrical pattern is the same in each one. Strophe means the 'turn' and antistrophe the 'turn back': the chorus dances one way across the *orkhēstra* as they sing the strophe and then the other way during the antistrophe. The speeches are in recitative: they are written in a tetrameter of one kind or another; by comparison with ordinary speech in Greek drama (iambic trimeters), the tetrameter form increases the tempo and animation of the delivery. The first speech, following the strophe, is termed the 'epirrhema', the second, following the antistrophe, the 'antepirrhema'.

In the agon, the chorus is usually clearly biased towards one side or the other and will either triumph with the side it supports or be won over by the opposing argument. By convention, the speaker who speaks second wins the contest. *Cavalry* has a second agon in addition to the first or 'main' agon; here, the first agon is referred to simply as 'the agon'.

The agon in *Cavalry* does not follow the regular structure; instead, almost the entire dramatic sequence is dialogue without long speeches, and very quickly it becomes a slanging match between Paphlagon and Agorakritos, who is supported throughout by Demosthenes. The chorus' participation shows a stronger adherence to their conventional role, with their odes dividing the agon into two sections of roughly equal length (303–81 and 382–460). As in the parodos (Chapter 3), the traditionalism of their role reflects their characterization as representatives of the Athenian elite, and Paphlagon and Agorakritos' destruction of poetic form reflects the chaotic nature of demagogic politics.

Both the chorus (277, 322–5) and Paphlagon (409) describe the agon as a contest in (Gk.) *anaideia*, which is usually translated as 'shamelessness' – whoever shows more *anaideia* wins. In view of the behaviour and attitudes of many characters in Aristophanes, it might be thought that this word for 'shamelessness' would be found frequently in his plays – indicating, for example, action or speech that would normally be embarrassing or disgraceful. In fact, *anaideia* is not common in Aristophanes: apart from the three instances in *Cavalry*, it is otherwise found only twice (*Clouds* 1236; fr. 238 Henderson). In view of the unusualness of this word in Aristophanes, the concentration of uses in *Cavalry* requires explanation.[1]

The standard translation of *anaideia* offered in the Greek lexicon, 'shamelessness' (LSJ *s.v.* I), does not describe the term's full meaning; indeed, there seems to be no single English word that captures it fully, though 'outrageousness' comes close.[2] In Herodotus (6.129.3-4), the Athenian Hippokleides at a banquet hosted by Cleisthenes, tyrant of Sicyon, dances in a headstand on a table waving his legs in the air; there, his behaviour is described as *anaideia*, and in that context it clearly means 'shamelessness'. By contrast, when the Greeks' refusal to retreat from Thermopylae strikes Xerxes as *anaideia*, the meaning must be closer to 'recklessness' (Herodotus 7.210.1). In the second century CE, the travel-writer Pausanias visited Athens and went to the hill known as the 'Areopagus', which served, among other functions, as a court for murder cases. He describes two rocks: for the accused the rock of 'Violence' (Gk. *Hybris*), and for the accuser the rock of *Anaideia*. Clearly the accuser was not 'shameless' but 'implacable' or 'without forgiveness'. In short, *anaideia* specifies actions, and the attitudes of mind behind them, as unmitigatedly extreme: shameless but also ruthless, reckless and unyielding – in fact, little short of insanity. The fragment of Aristophanes in which the word appears (fr. 238 Henderson) reads 'Oh, madness and *anaideia*!'

The agon in *Cavalry*, then, may be thought of as a competition in outrageousness of various kinds. It begins with the chorus attempting to impose order, dancing and singing the expected lyric ode (the strophe) that introduces the epirrhema (304-13). Their support for Agorakritos is unwavering and they attack Paphlagon, singing of his screaming that fills the whole earth, the assembly and the lawcourts

(304–5 cf. 311); of the political confusion he creates (309–10); and of his extortion and misappropriation of funds from the allied cities of Athenian empire (313). The themes of the demagogic voice, political turbulence and corruption are all familiar from earlier in the play.

After Agorakritos and Demosthenes describe how Paphlagon cheats customers who buy shoes from him (315–21), the chorus resumes their song (322–32) charging Paphlagon with the 'ruthlessness' (Gk. *anaideia*) with which he steals from foreigners (i.e. the allied cities of the empire). The chorus confirms the prediction of the oracle discovered in the prologue, that another man, even more repulsive than Paphlagon, has arisen to surpass him in corruption, audacity and (Gk.) *kobalikeumata* (330–2).

The word *kobalikeumata* is part of a cluster of words formed on the root *kobāl-* that are rare in what remains of ancient Greek. They are more prominent in *Cavalry* than anywhere else in Aristophanes: in fact, about half the known instances of this group of words in Greek comedy turn up in *Cavalry*, where they are always applied to either Paphlagon or Agorakritos (*Cavalry* 332, 417, 450, 635; *Frogs* 104, 1015. Cf. Pherecrates fr. 173 Storey; Phrynichus fr. 4a Storey). The word *kobalos*, which is vulgar and probably pre-Greek, seems originally to mean a 'baggage-carrier' or 'porter' (cf. Beekes *s.v.*). By the late fifth century it had become a pejorative, meaning a person who behaves and speaks like a baggage-carrier – at a guess, a slave or low-status freeman who enjoys antagonizing his social superiors with relatively passive forms of resistance, such as 'giving backchat' – much like Xanthias in *Frogs* or Karion in *Wealth*.

Translation into an insult in contemporary English, in which pejoratives rely heavily on sexual and scatological vocabulary, is difficult and can only be approximate. Archaisms like 'rogue' (LSJ *s.v.*) are surely less accurate than 'joker' or more insulting words like 'douchebag' or 'arsehole'. The cognate object nouns (i.e. what the *kobalos* says or does) must mean things like 'joking', 'trickery', 'graft', or 'bullshit'. In the parodos, the chorus accuses Paphlagon of 'total bullshit' (270) after he claims to intend to move a proposal for a monument to the cavalry on the acropolis. Later, Agorakritos (417) provides an example of a 'trick'

(Gk. *kobala*) that he once played (see below). The rarity of these words outside comedy suggests that they belong to a colloquial substrate of 'street language'. Their frequent appearance in *Cavalry* contributes to the characterization of Agorakritos and Paphlagon as 'lowlifes'. Notably, though Paphlagon is accused of such behaviour and accuses Agorakritos of it, only Agorakritos is happy to admit to it.

The chorus finishes their song by encouraging Agorakritos further. They tell him that he comes from where 'men who are real men' come (333) and must prove how useless it is to have a good upbringing (334). The remark about 'real men' marks a thematic development from the prologue scene, where Agorakritos did not think of himself as any kind of man at all. The chorus's phrase 'a good upbringing' uses language of the aristocratic values expressed by the Greek word *sōphrosynē* – literally 'sound-mindedness' – meaning moderation or self-control. The suggestion that this set of values is no longer any use in politics signals just how far the leadership of Athens has fallen. The replacement of *sōphrosynē* with an education like Agorakritos' (cf. 188–93) develops the theme of the social inversion.[3]

Paphlagon now tries to make a speech, as the structure of an agon requires, but Agorakritos repeatedly refuses to let him begin (336–40) and says he will fight to be allowed to speak *first* (338–9). This is a metatheatrical joke. There should be a speech at this point, spoken by the character who is going to lose the agon (i.e. Paphlagon), since the convention is that the second speaker wins. By stopping Paphlagon from speaking, Agorakritos wrecks the formal structure of the agon and turns it into a mudslinging match. Just as the oracle has predicted, he is a politician even more radical than Paphlagon.

Prevented from beginning a formal debate, Paphlagon asks what makes Agorakritos think he is capable of public-speaking (342), imagining condescendingly that the sausage-seller might have gained his inflated confidence from a victory in an easy lawsuit against a non-citizen (344–50). In Thucydides (3.38.6), Cleon criticizes the assembly for being full of men who want to think themselves capable of public speaking; if this was something that Cleon had said in the assembly and it was memorable,

Paphlagon's words would then remind the audience of Cleon's arrogant domination of assembly meetings (cf. Slater 2002: 73). In retort, Agorakritos asks how Paphlagon can think he has silenced the city with his speeches (351–2) – literally by 'having stuck your tongue down the throat of the polis'. The metaphor anticipates the way that Paphlagon will later present himself as a lover of Demos, suggesting that he forces his love of the people, which could otherwise be a positive image, on the city (for discussion of erotic themes in *Cavalry*, see Chapter 5).

From 353, Paphlagon and Agorakritos return to their contest in *anaideia*, by exchanging outrageous boasts; for example (353–60):

Paphlagon   Could you ever pit anyone against me? A man who will eat hot tuna steaks, and then, after drinking six pints of neat wine, cuss out[4] the generals in Pylos.

Agorakritos   I'll guzzle down beef tripe and pork belly and then, after draining the gravy and without washing my hands, I'll get hold of the politicians by the throat and throw Nicias into a panic.

Demosthenes   I liked most of what you said, but one thing doesn't sit right with me – that you're going to drain the gravy train all by yourself!

Their boasts are further examples of the metaphor of food as political power and success. Of note, too, in the passage translated above, is Demosthenes' corrupt greed (cf. 1255–6). The implication that even 'good' politicians are corrupt encourages the audience to think that Agorakritos will only prove even worse than Paphlagon, as the oracle has predicted, increasing the element of surprise at the end of the play.

The dialogue continues until Agorakritos abandons boasting and threatens to stuff Paphlagon's arse like a sausage-skin (364). As always Agorakritos is the first to plumb new depths of outrageousness, in this case moving from boasts to threats. Nothing in the text indicates it, but since he has yet to put down his knives (cf. 489), it is possible that Agorakritos menaces Paphlagon with the implements of his trade. When Demosthenes throws his weight behind Agorakritos once more (366), Paphlagon shifts the meter of his response into the short lines (iambic dimeters) of the pnigos, speeding up the pace of the dialogue and suggesting even greater fury (367). From this point, the end of the first phase of the agon moves towards cruder and more violent threats, culminating with Demosthenes' suggestion that they peg Paphlagon out like a pig for butchery and examine his anus – rather than the tongue, as would be the usual practice – to see if he has cysts indicating tapeworm (375–81).[5]

At 382 the chorus begins to dance and sing the antistrophe, opening the second half of the agon. Outrageousness (*anaideia*) is prominently thematized and the chorus appears shocked by the contest so far (382–5):

> **Chorus** It seems there really are things hotter than fire and more outrageous than the outrageous speeches made in the city!

The chorus continues to encourage Agorakritos, reminding him that Paphlagon is a coward (389–90). As in the first half of the agon, there is a short pause in the chorus' lyrics and Agorakritos accuses Paphlagon of stealing Demosthenes' victory at Pylos. The familiar imagery of success, in this case military victory, as food appears again here (391–4). Paphlagon replies with characteristically arrogant boasting: he has nothing to fear while the present council is in office and the Athenians sit in the assembly with their mouths hanging open, an image of stupidity (395–6; see Chapter 5). The continuation of the chorus's song makes the shamelessness of Paphlagon's words clear – nothing can make him blush (398–9). The mentions of the council and the assembly anticipate the plot development: after the agon, there will be contests before the council and then the assembly.

The chorus now swear an oath: 'If I do not hate you [Paphlagon], may I be turned into a fleece in the house of Cratinus and may I appear in a chorus in a tragedy by Morsimus!' (400–1). Aristophanes is fond of characterizing his rival Cratinus as an incontinent drunk (e.g. 535: see below on the parabasis; cf. *Peace* 700–3) and insulting the tragic writer Morsimus as a terrible poet (cf. *Peace* 802, *Frogs* 151). Hate is not a common emotion in Aristophanes (see Chapter 2), so the impassioned attitude of the chorus may have struck the audience as exceptional. The chorus finish their song wishing that Paphlagon might be forced to regurgitate the bribes he has taken (403–4; for the imagery, cf. *Acharnians* 6), whereupon they will sing a song of victory by Simonides: 'Drink! Drink! for these glad tidings' (406). Their poetic choice underlines, once more, the importance of foodstuffs as symbols of political triumph.[6]

Paphlagon's reaction confirms that the issue of the agon is not yet decided: he swears that Agorakritos shall not surpass him in *anaideia* (409). But ironically his oath introduces the sequence in which Agorakritos will conclusively outdo him. In a dialogue with Demosthenes, Agorakritos describes one of his 'bullshit tricks' (Gk. *kobala*, 417): when he was a boy, he would distract the butchers so that he could steal their meat, hide it between his buttocks and swear innocence by the gods (417–24). This, he claims, led a politician to declare that he would one day become leader of the people (425–6). Nothing in the text indicates it, but it is possible that the actor playing Agorakritos could stuff his large comic costume phallus back between his legs in a visual demonstration of this trick. Agorakritos' story gives Demosthenes the opening for the standard Aristophanic joke that politicians are the passive sexual partners of other men: it is the mark of every successful Athenian politician to steal and then swear a false oath with another man's meat in his anus (427–8).

Paphlagon is momentarily stumped for a response, other than calling this 'audacity' (*thrasus*: 429): he is beginning to lose his grip in the contest and be outdone in outrageousness (cf. Henderson 1991: 69 on the mildness of Paphlagon's language in *Cavalry* by comparison with Agorakritos). He adopts a new metaphor: he will sweep his adversaries away like a hurricane – another example of the theme of chaos and confusion (431: Gk. *tarattein*; see Chapter 5). His words introduce a series of nautical metaphors, ending with Paphlagon, in defeat, offering his opponents a bribe, which they accept (439–41).

Figuring the city as a ship ('the ship of state') is conventional in ancient Greek literature and would have been fully familiar to the audience (e.g. Alcaeus fr. 326 Campbell). Agorakritos and Demosthenes trim the sails and keep the ship afloat (432–4, 436–7, 440–1), while Paphlagon becomes the storm threatening to sink them – a powerful image of the dangerous turbulence in Athenian politics under Cleon (Edmunds 1987a: 6–16, 1987b: 233–47; Whitman 1964: 90–2.) but also one that suggests Agorakritos' growing ability to assume the leadership of the city.

Paphlagon's storm carries him again into beginning the pnigos, with which the second part of the agon closes. There is a flurry of threats, accusations and insults (442–50), with Agorakritos successfully capping Paphlagon each time. Lines 445–9 contain two accusations concerning ancestry that require explanation:

Paphlagon   I declare you are descended from the family cursed by Athene.

Agorakritos   And I declare your grandfather was one of the guardsmen . . . of Hippias' wife, Leather . . . I mean Heather!

First, Paphlagon accuses Agorakritos of having accursed ancestry (445–6). The reference is to an unsuccessful attempt by Cylon to establish a tyranny in Athens in the late seventh century. After the attempt failed, Cylon's followers, who had taken refuge in the sanctuary of Athene Polias on the acropolis, were murdered by members of the aristocratic Alcmaeonid family. The murderers and their descendants were held to be cursed (cf. Herodotus 5.71; Thucydides 1.126). This had become a live issue just before the outbreak of the Peloponnesian War when the Spartans had called on the Athenians to drive out 'the accursed', which included the Athenian leader Pericles, who had maternal descent from the Alcmaeonids. The Spartans intended to have Pericles, Athens' leading politician and a strong proponent of war, banished or at least lose his public standing with the Athenians, who might then be more inclined to make concessions (Thucydides 1.127). Paphlagon's accusation is ludicrous, since Agorakritos is descended from the lowest sort of people (cf. 185–6); but ironically it might encourage the audience to think of Agorakritos as a leader like Pericles – this serves as another harbinger of Agorakritos' triumph over Paphlagon.

Agorakritos' response is to accuse Paphlagon of association with the last tyrant of Athens, Hippias, alleging that his grandfather was one of the bodyguards of Hippias' wife Myrsine; the charge is made with a

ridiculous pun on her name evoking Cleon's tannery (449). It is possible
that Cleon was related, though only by marriage, to the family of
Harmodios, one of the two 'tyrannicides' who assassinated Hipparchus,
Hippias' brother, in 514 BCE, and in popular imagination brought
democracy to Athens. If so, the joke about Cleon's grandfather would
have all the more bite if Cleon had tried to make political capital out of
a tenuous family connection. Notably, Aristophanes makes fun of
Cleon in another context involving Harmodios in *Wasps* (1224–7).[7]

After Paphlagon and Agorakritos trade more insults (450: 'You're a
bullshitter!' 'You're a psycho!') the action of the agon concludes when,
with Demosthenes' encouragement, Agorakritos beats Paphlagon into
submission (451–6) – a final and physical demonstration of Agorakritos'
greater outrageousness. The chorus announces the outcome of the agon
by congratulating Agorakritos (457–60): they hail him as the 'Best and
most nobly-born chunk of meat!' and call him 'saviour of our city and its
citizens' (457–8). Their words add to the theme of social inversion – the
aristocratic value of noble birth is confounded with Agorakritos' origins
among the lowest of Athenian citizens and his despised trade as a butcher.
Furthermore, they confirm Agorakritos' role as the comic hero in the
'salvation' (Gk. *sōtēria*) pattern of the comic plot (see Chapter 3): in the
prologue, Demosthenes and Nicias wanted a way of escape for themselves;
here, the prospect has broadened to encompass the whole city.

Episode (461–97)

After the agon there is a short episode. Paphlagon accuses his adversaries
of conspiracy, describing their plot as bolted and glued together, using
carpentry as a metaphor (463). Agorakritos replies by accusing Paphlagon
of intriguing with Argos, but his accusations lack a metaphor and
Demosthenes asks why he is not saying anything 'out of the wagon-
makers' workshop' (464). It is of note that the use of an appropriately
framed metaphor is more important than a concrete accusation of
treachery (465–7), suggesting that Athenian political discourse has

degenerated into cheap point-scoring. Agorakritos catches on quickly and accuses Paphlagon of welding his plot together, introducing a metaphor from the bronze foundry (468–70). The exchange of trade metaphors is another exercise in rhetorical inventiveness, in which Agorakritos proves more than a match for Paphlagon. Again, it may reflect Cleon's real-life rhetoric, if his self-fashioning in the assembly involved presenting himself as a tradesman from among the masses (see Chapter 2).

Defeated in this latest rhetorical contest, Paphlagon threatens to go to the council and denounce his adversaries for plotting with some of Athens' enemies (475–9). As he exits (481), Demosthenes urges Agorakritos to run after him. Agorakritos puts down his tripe and knives (488–9) and Demosthenes readies him for what is figured as first a wrestling bout and then a cockfight (490–7). The images of one-to-one combat evoke the violence of demagogic politics.

At the end of the episode, Demosthenes exits the stage (497). His disappearance is necessary for the performance of the parabasis, since the convention is that the chorus are left alone on stage, and because the actor playing Demosthenes must return as Demos. Demosthenes' absence is an indication of Agorakritos' growing self-confidence in his battle with Paphlagon: until now, he has largely taken direction from Demosthenes; but from this point forward, he will grapple with his adversary with only the support of the chorus (cf. Slater 2002: 74–5).

Parabasis (498–610)

The parabasis (a conventional element of Old Comedy, found in its most developed form in Aristophanes' earlier plays) fills the dramatic time during which Paphlagon and Agorakritos are offstage addressing the council. Later in the play, there is a second parabasis (see Chapter 7). In plays containing two parabases, the first parabasis is often referred to simply as 'the parabasis', just as the first agon is usually referred to as 'the agon'.

There are two sections in a first parabasis. After a short prelude (Gk. *kommation*) sung by the chorus, there is an extensive speech from the *koryphaios* (i.e. the 'chorus-leader').[8] The speech is an address to the audience on behalf of the poet. The speaker makes his address after stepping apart from the rest of the chorus. This action gives the parabasis its name because the Greek word *parabasis* means a 'step to the side'. The cognate verb, (Gk. *parabainein*) 'step aside', is often used metatheatrically to refer to the parabasis (*Cavalry* 508; cf. *Acharnians* 629, *Peace* 735). In the chorus-leader's address, the anapaestic meter is conventional, to the extent that Aristophanes refers metatheatrically to this part of the parabasis as 'the anapaests' (*Cavalry* 504; cf. *Acharnians* 627, *Peace* 735; *Birds* 684). The chorus-leader's anapaests close with a pnigos or 'choker' (see Chapter 3).

The second section of a parabasis is an 'epirrhematic syzygy', a poetic structure that has been described above (in the section on the agon). It is generally held that the speeches (the epirrhema and antepirrhema) were delivered by the chorus-leader, but it is possible that the chorus divided into two, each hemi-chorus taking one speech. In contrast to 'the anapaests', which are delivered on behalf of the poet, the epirrhema and antepirrhema are spoken by the chorus in character. Like 'the anapaests', the two speeches are recitative: they are written in long verses of trochaic tetrameters, a meter that, by comparison with passages of speech (in iambic trimeters), increases the tempo and animation of the delivery. Five motifs are conventional in an Aristophanic parabasis (cf. Imperio 2004: 22–99): praise for the poet and defence against criticisms of him; praise for the chorus; an appeal for the audience's favour; ridicule of named individuals; and invocations of the gods.

In *Cavalry*, the parabasis has a conventional structure, reflecting once more the traditionalism of the chorus of aristocratic cavalrymen. In the short prelude (498–506), the chorus bid Agorakritos farewell as he leaves the stage for his clash with Paphlagon in the council chamber. With Agorakritos sent on his way, the chorus turn to the audience and encourage them to pay attention to 'the anapaests' (503–6).

The chorus-leader steps forward to address the audience (cf. 508) and begins the anapaests (507–11):

If any comic director from the past had tried to make us approach the audience to address them with a speech, he would not have achieved it easily. But now, this poet has earned it because he hates the same men we do, he dares to say what is just, and he does battle nobly against Typhon the hurricane!

The purpose of the anapaests in *Cavalry* is for Aristophanes to win the audience's sympathies and – tongue in cheek – to promote himself as the greatest comic poet Athens has ever seen. The strategy, as is usual in Aristophanes' parabases, is defensive, in contrast to the friendly and complimentary demeanour that is usual elsewhere (cf. 228, 233). In the parabasis, the poet says he tries his hardest, but the audience is likely to let him down. In his bid for victory, Aristophanes presents himself as a friend of both the elite and the mass of Athenian citizens – represented, in this speech, by the elite cavalry and the mass of trireme rowers. The fundamental unity of mass and elite in Athens is a theme that connects the various elements of the parabasis.

The opening lines of the anapaests (quoted above) assert Aristophanes' poetic genius: it would not have been easy for any other comic poet to persuade cavalrymen to deliver a parabasis (508). The *koryphaios* lists the reasons that the chorus supports Aristophanes (509–11): he hates the same people that they do (i.e. Cleon and his supporters); he speaks the truth to power (cf. *Acharnians* 501); and he advances nobly against his terrifying opponent. The word for 'nobly' (511: Gk. *gennaiōs*) aligns Aristophanes with the elite, for whom noble birth was an essential part of their identity; the same word is used later in the parabasis by the chorus to describe how they defend their city (577). The characterization of Cleon as Typhon (511), a monster with one hundred heads who, in myth, is the father of storms (Hesiod, *Theogony* 821–35, 869–80), fits the thematic pattern of associating Paphlagon (and therefore Cleon) with images of disturbance and chaos (see Chapter 5). The monstrosity of the adversary (cf. *Wasps* 1031–7; *Peace* 752–60) suggests that Aristophanes' comic poetry is commensurately heroic.

The centrepiece of the *koryphaios'* speech explains why Aristophanes has only now begun to direct the plays that he writes. This passage contains some of the most important evidence for Aristophanes' early career. Aristophanes' first three plays (*Banqueters* in 428/7; *Babylonians* in 427/6; and *Acharnians* in 426/5) were directed for him by his fellow demesman Callistratus.[9] The reasons for Aristophanes' hesitancy are given as follows: first, directing comedy is difficult and success is highly uncertain (516); second, the audience soon grows tired of even the most successful comic poets, as the careers of Magnes, Crates and Cratinus are alleged to show (518–41); and third, it was essential for Aristophanes to learn the ropes of comic directing one by one (541–4). The succession of comic poets with Aristophanes implicitly the fourth, who will surpass his forerunners Magnes, Crates and Cratinus, may reflect the oracular prediction of a fourfold succession of demagogues (128–43; see Chapter 3); this aligns Aristophanes with his hero Agorakritos as a comic saviour of the city from Cleon (cf. Hubbard 1991: 77–8).

Aristophanes' description of the careers of Magnes, Cratinus and Crates (see further, Biles 2011: 100–9) deserves investigation. He claims all three have ended in failure. It is likely that by this time Magnes and Crates had ceased producing comic drama, but what is probably Cratinus' last play, *Wineskin*, won first prize at the Dionysia in 423 BCE, the year after Aristophanes' *Cavalry* – in short, Aristophanes' reports of the death of Cratinus' comedy are greatly exaggerated.

In the case of each predecessor, Aristophanes is concerned to remind the audience how cruel their treatment of comic poets is: Magnes was driven from the stage (525); there is no pity for Cratinus (531); and Crates endured the audience's anger and abuse (537). Notably, the long mid-section of the speech (514–41) exhibits the feature of ring-composition – a poetic structure in which a theme appears at the beginning of a poem or passage of poetry and then again at the end. The effect is heavily emphatic; here, the purpose of the ring composition is to emphasize the difficulty of pleasing Athenian audiences with a performance of comedy.

Magnes was probably producing comedy from the 470s down to the 430s. He was highly successful, winning at least eleven victories. Therefore, as far as we know, he won many more victories than

Aristophanes. Aristophanes' description of Magnes' brand of comedy (520–5) suggests that he was musically inventive and memorably used animal choruses (as Aristophanes does in *Birds* for example). The report that in his dotage Magnes' comedy 'lost its sense of humour' and that Magnes was driven off the stage (524–5), may be a comment about Magnes' approach to writing comic drama. Aristophanes' use of the Greek word *skōptein* (to describe where Magnes fell short) implies insults or *ad hominem* invective. This suggests that Aristophanes' brand of comedy (political satire and personal insult) has been shown to be superior – a quietly self-congratulatory implication.[10]

Cratinus is treated with the most extensive assessment (526–36). His career probably lasted from the 450s to the 420s. Cratinus' poetry is described as like a river in flood (for the imagery, see Hubbard 1991: 74 with n. 35), washing away everything in its path including his enemies (527–8). This suggests a lack of subtlety but also a style close to the kind of comedy Aristophanes wrote, one based on topical satire and lampooning prominent individuals. Aristophanes' praise for Cratinus is considerably greater than for Magnes and Crates. Once, he writes, Cratinus was so popular that at symposia (drinking parties) only his songs would be sung (529–30); but now he is like a broken lyre and wanders about like Konnos, wearing an old and dried out garland (534). The latter implies that Cratinus' poetic victories were long in the past: Aristophanes had defeated Cratinus at the Lenaea the previous year with *Acharnians*, which beat Cratinus' play *Tempest-Tossed*.[11] Ironically, Konnos was one of Cratinus' comic victims (fr. 349 Storey). He was a famous Olympic victor in music who taught Socrates the lyre (e.g. Plato, *Euthydemus* 272c), but he appears to have declined into poverty and alcoholism in his later years.

Addiction to wine is a charge Aristophanes enjoyed levelling at Cratinus (cf. *Peace* 702–3), probably in response to Cratinus' own poetic self-fashioning in his plays (Bakola 2010: 16–24 with further literature). Cratinus turned Aristophanes' allegations to victorious use in his comedy *Wineskin*, performed the year after *Cavalry*. *Wineskin* was a satire of its author's alcoholic incontinence: though being married to Comedy (personified), Cratinus takes to drink (Bakola 2010: 59–63).

The play won the comic competition at the City Dionysia in 423 BCE, beating Aristophanes' *Clouds* into third place. Finally, Aristophanes gives Cratinus a couple of backhanded compliments. He is worthy of the honour of *drinking* at public expense in the Prytaneion (the usual honour was dining!); and of *watching* performances from the front-row seats in the theatre, implying again that he is no longer capable of producing comedy (535–6).[12]

The career of Crates is given the briefest of summaries (537–40): his style of comedy is described as refined but somewhat insubstantial, in clear contrast to the description of Cratinus. His plays are believed to date from the 450s to the 430s. About a century later, Aristotle (*Poetics* 1449b7-9) writes that Crates was the first Athenian comic poet to abandon the 'iambic' style of comedy (i.e. personal invective) and compose 'stories and plots'. This might mean that Crates' comedy was closer to that of Menander, the preeminent comic poet of Aristotle's day, who wrote comedies of that kind. It is of note that the surviving fragments of Crates preserve no certain example of personal invective. Therefore, Crates contrasts with Cratinus, who is particularly associated with the 'iambic' style of comedy. The nature of Crates' style of comedy and the precise meaning of Aristotle's comment on it remain uncertain, but what matters here is that Aristophanes is focused, above all, on the attitude of the audience to Crates: eventually he met with irritation and abuse (537).[13]

As we have noted in the case of each comic poet, Aristophanes mentions the poor treatment they have been given by the fickle Athenian audience (518): this is what has made him bide his time before beginning to direct comic drama (541). The *koryphaios* describes the development of Aristophanes' career, from writer to director, in a nautical metaphor: first he had to learn to row, then to be a lookout, and only finally to take the helm. The metaphor is surely designed to appeal to a large part of the audience: Aristophanes aligns himself with the 'thetes' (Gk. *thētes*), the lowest class of citizens, many of whom were rowers on Athenian triremes.

Having sought sympathy for Aristophanes through recounting the failures of other comic poets, the chorus-leader asks the audience to shout out and clap for the poet, so that he will achieve his objective, win the Lenaea competition and leave the theatre with his forehead gleaming – a self-effacing reference from Aristophanes to his early baldness (cf. *Peace* 767–74). He asks for shouting and applause with another nautical metaphor (546): the audience are to use eleven oars, perhaps meaning their ten fingers plus the tongue (Sommerstein 1981: 173).[14] The choice of words, again, seems likely to have appealed to trireme-rowers in the audience. Striking a note of popular appeal here balances Aristophanes' claim, at the beginning of the anapaests, to enjoy the favour of the elite.

In the second part of the *parabasis* there are two strophic choral odes, each followed by a speech. The strophe is an invocation of the god Poseidon, summoning him in support of the chorus (559). They call on him as Poseidon god of horses (551–3) and the sea (554–5). Symbolically, then, Poseidon is the god whose worship is shared by the equestrian elite, who had the wealth to keep horses, serve in the cavalry, compete in chariot races, and so on (556–8), but also of the mass of thetes who rowed for their living on Athens' triremes (554–5). The symbolic significance of the worship of Poseidon as a unifying force for Athenians (cf. Hubbard 1991: 80) is emphasized again in the appellations 'dearest of the gods to Phormion' and 'dearest of all the gods to the Athenians these days' (562–4). Phormion was a popular and successful commander, especially at sea – again, a unifying figure held in high esteem by both the Athenian elite (including the cavalry) and the masses (including rowers).[15]

The first speech, strictly interpreted, is delivered in praise of the bravery of the chorus's fathers (565). However, the emphasis on victory on land and at sea (567) here avoids explicit mention of the cavalry (cf. Edmunds 1987b: 253–4), and the chorus's words are sufficiently vague that 'our fathers' could also be understood to refer to the ancestors of everyone in the theatre, again establishing shared interests between chorus and spectators. In this ode, as in the following one, a humorous remark is made about someone close to Cleon, in this case his father Kleainetos (574). The joke (573–6) seems to be that Cleon has only been able to obtain the privilege of *sitēsis* by having his father propose the decree granting it – in other words, no independent proposer would support Cleon's application for civic honours following his victory at Pylos (cf. Osborne 1981: 169–70).

The last lines of the speech (576–80) are a request from the chorus on their own behalf: since they protect the land without asking reward (in contrast to a commander like Cleon), they should not incur resentment in peacetime for the aristocratic trait of growing their hair long. The chorus' masks surely had long hair (cf. 1121–2). This was a fashion popular among wealthy Athenians with equestrian pursuits (e.g. *Clouds* 14, 545; *Wasps* 466), but it was widely regarded with hostility and suspicion of antidemocratic sentiments by ordinary Athenians (cf. Lysias 16.18; Donlan 1999: 161). There is an apparent contrast here, too, with the demos, which continually demands pay (e.g. 945; Wohl 2002: 109); but since the cavalry received public financial support (Chapter 2), their selfless patriotism may be taken with a grain of salt.

The antistrophe is an appeal for victory for Athens in the war against the Peloponnesians and for Aristophanes at the Lenaea. The chorus invokes 'Athene the guardian of the city' (Gk. *Pallas Polioukhos*) and 'protectress of the land' (Gk. *medeousa khōras*), asking that she bring the goddess Nike ('Victory') with her (581, 585, 589). The audience would surely be reminded, here, of the chryselephantine statue of Athene in the Parthenon holding Nike in the palm of her hand. The goddess is asked to bestow victory on 'these men' (592), another subtly ambiguous expression (cf. Hubbard 1991: 81) that could mean 'on the chorus' or 'on everyone in the theatre', with the appropriate kind of victory – poetic or military – for each. The second epithet used of Athene, (Gk.) *medeousa khōras* (cf. 763), is the title under which the goddess was worshipped in the subject states of the Athenian Empire (Sommerstein 1997: 184): its imperialist tone reinforces the impression of shared nationalist sentiment between elite and mass that the strophe projected (cf. Edmunds 1987b: 255–6).

The pairing of Poseidon and Athene in the two lyric odes of the parabasis is surely no accident, for in myth these two gods had once competed with one another to become Athens' tutelary deity. Athene triumphed with the gift of the olive tree, defeating Poseidon's gift of the horse (see Bowie 1993: 66–7). Although Poseidon lost the contest, he and Athene were both honoured on the acropolis, the most sacred space in Athens, and Poseidon retained a place in Athenian religion second only to Athene herself. In 421 BCE, not many years after the production of *Cavalry*, the Athenians began to construct a temple, the Erechtheum (also on the acropolis), in which Athene and Poseidon were honoured together. The mythical rivalry between the two deities and their special significance to Athenians was long established; here, it seems, once more, to emphasize the essential unity of mass and elite in Athens, whatever political divisions might arise between them (cf. Bowie 1993: 66–74). Dover (1972: 99) suggests that, here and elsewhere in *Cavalry*, Aristophanes seeks to establish 'a sentimental unity of classes against leaders like Cleon'.

The whimsical tone of the second speech creates a contrast with the first. The chorus praise their horses for their service in battles and in the Peloponnesian invasions of Attica (595–7), for the cavalry was routinely sent out to harass invaders (cf. Thucydides 2.19.2, 22.2; 3.1.2). Then, fantastically, they imagine their horses rowing transport ships in an amphibious expedition (601), an image that unites the efforts of the elite cavalry and the mass of thetes. The horses beach their ships at Corinth (604), make camp and forage for food – in this case crabs (605–6). The amphibious attack on Corinth involving the cavalry alludes to a recent event: the previous year (425 BCE), Nicias had led an expedition, in which two-hundred cavalry participated, ferried to Corinth on horse-transport ships (Thucydides 4.42-4). The heroics of the cavalry in the battle at Solygeia, where they had been instrumental in routing the Corinthians and killing their general (Thucydides 4.44.1-2), contrast with Cleon's undeserved and self-aggrandizing victory at Pylos. Their victory at Solygeia is perhaps the reference behind Paphlagon's earlier promise of a monument to the cavalry in honour of their bravery (266–8).

There is also a joke at the expense of one of Cleon's close associates, Theoros. This man was follower of Cleon, well known for his excessively obsequious behaviour (cf. *Wasps* 42–51, 418–19, 599–600, 1236–42). Aristophanes makes fun of him in *Acharnians* (134–66) as an

incompetent ambassador, given to drinking heavily (*Acharnians* 141).
The chorus imagines Theoros overhearing a Corinthian crab's dismay at
being utterly unable to escape the Athenian cavalry (608–10):

> **Chorus**   … Theoros said that a Corinthian crab said:
> 'Truly terrible it is, Poseidon, if neither in the deep,
> nor by land nor sea, can I escape the cavalry!'

The crab's words are a parody of a popular drinking song by the lyric
poet Timocreon (fr. 731 Campbell): 'Blind Wealth, it would have been
better if you had appeared neither on land nor by sea nor on the
continent [i.e. Asia]' (i.e. anywhere in the world). Evidently Aristophanes
was fond of it, since he also parodies it in *Acharnians* 533–4.

The point of the joke about Theoros has been much debated,
beginning with the ancient commentators, who tried to explain it in
various ways (Σ 608). They claim, without evidence, that Theoros was
ridiculed in comedy as a gluttonous devotee of seafood, which would
explain how he heard what a crab had to say about the cavalry, and
gourmandizing would fit well with Theoros' alleged overindulgence in
wine. But the scholiasts also point out that Theoros says that the crab
referred to 'the cavalry', not 'the horses', and that this is, therefore, an
attempt at flattering the Athenian cavalry. This seems to be the most
likely explanation of the joke: the important words are: 'Theoros *said*
that a crab *said* …' (608). Much as Paphlagon tried to flatter the chorus
in the parodos (266–8), Theoros tries to ingratiate himself with the
cavalry with a smarmy compliment (i.e. that the Athenian cavalry are
an invincible military unit wherever they go in the world). A closely
parallel example of ridicule of Theoros is found in *Acharnians* (142–
50), where he tells the assembly a flattering tale of the Thracian king
Sitakles' devotion to Athens. Thematically, Theoros' obsequiousness
anticipates the second half of the play, where Paphlagon and Agorakritos
compete in a contest to flatter Demos.[16]

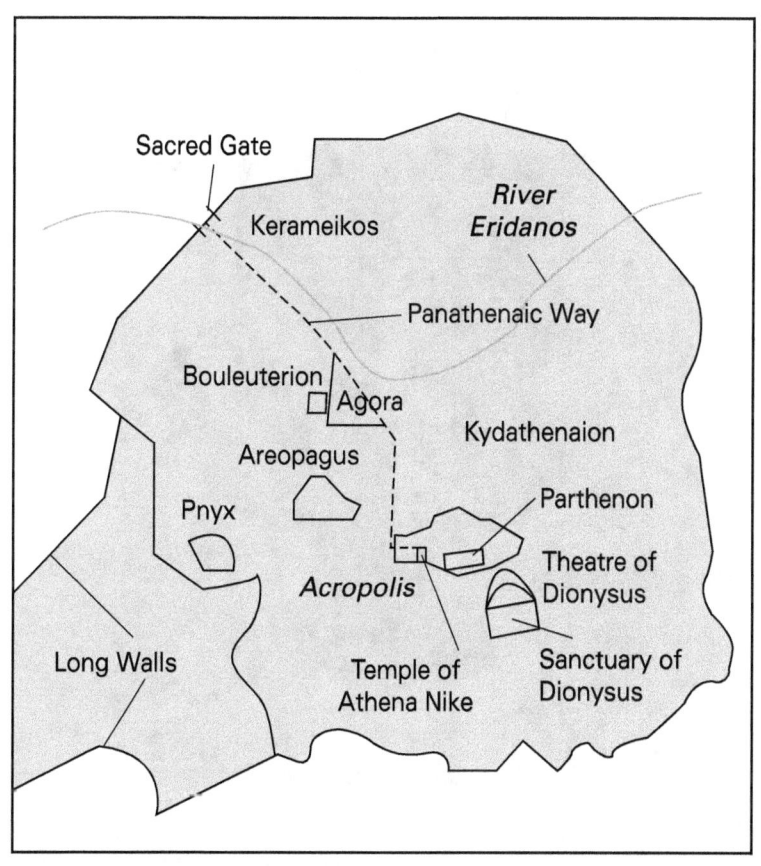

Figure 1 Map of ancient Athens (not to scale).

Figure 2 Apulian red-figure krater, *c*. 400–390 BCE, formerly attributed to the Tarporley Painter, more recently attributed to the Dolon Painter (New York, Metropolitan Museum of Art 24.97.104).

Figure 3 Athenian black-figure amphora, *c.* 550–500 BCE (Berlin, Antikensammlung F 1697, © Antikensammlung, Staatliche Museen zu Berlin – Preußischer Kulturbesitz. Photograph: Johannes Laurentius).

Figure 4 Athenian black-figure amphora, *c.* 575–525 BCE (Rome, Museo Gregoriano Etrusco Vaticano 17829, © Governorate of the Vatican City State-Directorate of the Vatican Museums).

5

Cavalry 611–996: Report of Off-Stage Action and Second Agon

The central sequence of *Cavalry* showcases two different comic 'type-scenes': a report of offstage action and a second agon. Agorakritos' narrative of his victory in the council chamber is remarkable for being one of the longest descriptions of offstage action in Aristophanes and the longest, by far, to be delivered as an uninterrupted monologue.

The second agon is a competition to become Demos' lover. Agorakritos defeats Paphlagon with generous gifts. In return he receives Demos' signet-ring, another step on his journey to become Athens' preeminent demagogue. Beaten once more, Paphlagon demands a contest in reciting oracles before the assembly and the chorus sings a short ode ridiculing Cleon.

Episode (611–755)

To the relief of the anxious chorus (612), Agorakritos returns successful from his competition with Paphlagon for the goodwill of the council. The chorus's song introduces a long narrative speech from Agorakritos, creating in the imagination of the audience two spaces that are not represented on stage, the marketplace and the council chamber (for a map, see Figure 1). In theatre theory, these imaginary, offstage locations are known as 'diegetic space', since they are *narrated* to the audience, not represented on stage (Issacharoff 1981).

Diegetic space is a well-established element of ancient Greek drama. It is often found in tragedy, especially in the type-scene known as the 'messenger speech', in which a messenger or herald brings a report of action that cannot easily be staged: for instance, a battle or more frequently a gruesome death. But comedy, too, knows the narration of offstage action.

Agorakritos' narration (624–82) is, in one respect, unique in Aristophanes: it is, by far, the longest uninterrupted narrative of offstage action found in any play. Elsewhere, only Karion's narrative in *Wealth* (627–770) is more extensive, but it is a dialogue in which Karion is merely the main speaker. Among the other significant passages reporting offstage action in Aristophanes, only one (*Birds* 1119–63) is more than half the length of Agorakritos' narrative, and it is, again, a dialogue. Moreover, in *Wealth*, Karion's elaborate narrative, like many other shorter narrative speeches in Aristophanes, clearly parodies the tragic messenger speech. The same has usually been held for Agorakritos' narrative (cf. Landfester 1967: 45–6, esp. n. 130), but in fact it is remarkable, among other Aristophanic 'messenger' speeches, for the relative absence of tragic parody: it is in fact the closest thing to purely comic reportage that we find anywhere in Aristophanes.

The unusual nature of Agorakritos' speech is emphasized by the words of the chorus immediately before it: his absence has worried them (612) and they ask for news of his latest clash with Paphlagon (614). When he tells them he has won (615), they sing the strophe of a strophic ode, expressing their joy and eagerness to hear what he has to say (616–23); this will be answered at the end of Agorakritos' speech with the antistrophe (683–90). The framing of an episode in a strophic choral structure is seldom found in Aristophanes; it reflects the special dramatic quality of an episode in which an actor, alone on stage, delivers an extensive speech to the chorus (cf. *Acharnians* 490–571).

In outline, Agorakritos' narrative runs as follows (624–82). He arrived at the council chamber just after Paphlagon, who had already begun accusing the cavalry of a conspiracy. With a parodic prayer, Agorakritos burst into the council chamber and yelled out that he had seen that sardines were on sale for the best price since the outbreak of the war. The council lost interest in Paphlagon and hung on Agorakritos' every word. Paphlagon proposed a large public sacrifice in thanks for the news, but Agorakritos outdid him with a proposal for much larger sacrifices. As Paphlagon was being dragged off, he begged the council to listen to a proposal of peace from Sparta; but with cheap sardines on sale, the council was happy to let the war go on. Before the councillors could leave the chamber to go to the market, Agorakritos ran ahead and bought up all the vegetables and herbs needed to season the fish, so that he could make a gift of them to the council and win even greater praise.

From this perspective, it becomes clear that Agorakritos' speech is, in essence, a report of an agon held offstage. In form, it reflects the loose structure of the play's two agons (see Chapter 4 and below). Paphlagon speaks first, as is conventional for the agonist who will eventually lose, Agorakritos responds, and the council assumes the role of the chorus, who, at first, incline towards Paphlagon but are won over by Agorakritos. Since *Cavalry* stages a second as well as a first agon, there is no room for another, because, as a rule, Aristophanes' plays include one agon, or two, or none. In effect, then, this episode creates space for a third agon, by locating it offstage. *Cavalry* is Aristophanes' most 'agonistic' play: most of the stage action (273–1253) can be thought of as an extended agon, with two characters disputing an issue before the chorus. The agonistic quality of Agorakritos' narrative is hinted at in the chorus' words when they ask Agorakritos what happened: 'Tell us how you contested the matter' (614). The verse contains two metatheatrical jokes: first, the word for 'tell', (Gk.) *aggellein*, alludes to the type-scene in which a messenger, (Gk.) *aggelos*, delivers a narrative speech; second, the word for 'contested', (Gk.) *agōnizein*, hints that Agorakritos' report will contain a narrative of an agon.

In terms of the shape of the play, Agorakritos' victory before the council is the second in the series of three main victories over Paphlagon, each occurring in a larger and more public political forum than the last. The first is a struggle among generals and demagogues, with Demosthenes bringing in a new ally: it may be thought of as a high-level and relatively private deliberation between some of the most powerful men in the city – perhaps like the meetings of the ten annually-elected generals (Gk. *stratēgoi*). The contest before the council of 500 reported here is a much

larger and more public venue. The third and final victory, once Demos
appears on stage, will be in the democratic assembly itself.

The audience's interest in Agorakritos' speech is engaged in various
ways. Like the messenger speeches of Greek tragedy, Agorakritos'
narrative is poetically captivating because it makes use of unusual
vocabulary, some of it very surprising in the mouth of a character like
Agorakritos. It is also entertaining because of the satirical description
of how the council is won over with the availability of cheap fish.

Surprising poetic vocabulary appears immediately that Agorakritos
reports his arrival at the council chamber. He entered just after
Paphlagon, who began a speech 'bursting forth thunderous words,
saying ludicrous things and hurling mountains; he bombarded the
cavalry, calling them conspirators in most persuasive terms' (624–9).
This description of Paphlagon's rhetoric grabs the audience's attention
with several high-flown poetic words, perhaps modelled on the poet
Pindar.[1] The effect of Paphlagon's persuasiveness is expressed in two
striking images (629–31): the councillors' faces became pale as he filled
them with the 'the orach of his lies' (orach is an herb that was believed
in antiquity to be capable of draining the colour from the face); and
'they looked mustard' (i.e. their faces took on the expression of someone
eating the mustard plant) and their brows furrowed (i.e. with the
eyebrows raised, perhaps in shock). The Greek words for orach and the
mustard plant are very rare, even in the remains of comedy, where food
words are common. Moreover, the portmanteau 'false-orach' is only
found here ancient Greek and may be an Aristophanic coinage. The
rare words and the surprising metaphors used here and elsewhere in
this speech underline Agorakritos' characteristic resourcefulness.[2]

Seeing that Paphlagon was persuading the councillors with his
trickery (632–3), Agorakritos tells the chorus that he prayed to a
catalogue of unfamiliar deities for the qualities needed to combat
Paphlagon: outrageousness (see Chapter 4), daring, and skill in speaking
(634–8). His humorously parodic prayer invokes a catalogue of obscure
'divinities' (634–6). Some of them may, in fact, be supernatural figures
of myths or a stratum of popular belief lost to us. However, since several

of the words Agorakritos uses here reappear in *Wealth* 279–80, where they are simply insults thrown by the chorus at the slave Karion, it is possible that Agorakritos has inventively personified them as though they were gods, as the scholiast thought (Σ 634). Knowledge of classical Greek vocabulary, even where it is not literary (as it is in tragedy, for example), is heavily skewed, not only towards the language of the social elite, but also to the language that social elites used in formal rather than informal contexts (e.g. lawcourt speeches): in short, it is highly sanitized. Since Agorakritos' words are rare even in comedy, where plenty of rude words are to be found, they may derive from a kind of 'street' Greek, fully appropriate to Agorakritos' character.

Agorakritos' parodic prayer is answered from somewhere in the divine realm with a favourable omen – a man with a (sexually) enlarged anus farts on the right, the side of good omens, portending Agorakritos' victory; the 'fart joke' is funny because the usual good omen was a sneeze on the righthand side (cf. Plutarch *Themistocles* 13.2). In response, Agorakritos tells the chorus, he prostrated himself on the ground in obeisance (639–40); then, after breaking down the barrier that kept the public out of the council chamber by using his backside, he opened his mouth wide and bellowed at the council (640–2). The phrase 'dashing my arse against it, I broke down the barrier' (640–1) is a good illustration of a widespread technique of Aristophanic humour – the juxtaposition of discordant lexical registers. The verb (Gk.) *theinein* ('dash', 'hurl' etc.) is elevated and poetic (it is used often in Homer and tragedy) and sounds ridiculous when linked to the coarse word Agorakritos uses for his backside (Gk. *prōktos*).

The next part of Agorakritos' narrative describes what happened once he was inside the council chamber. He says he bawled out good news from the marketplace: 'I have never seen sardines at a better price since the war broke out!', i.e. in 431 BCE, seven years earlier (642–5). The council at once became calm, like the sea after a storm; again, Aristophanes uses a very rare word (Gk. *diagalēnizein*), found only here in ancient Greek, to construct a remarkable metaphor. Agorakritos' calming effect opposes the storm that Paphlagon, characteristically, had raised in the council chamber (cf. 626). Whereas earlier Agorakritos had had to weather the storm (430–41), now he is able to counteract its effects, another step on the way to victory over Paphlagon.

Agorakritos reports (642) that he began his speech with the proper formal address to the council (Gk. *ō boulē*). At the Dionysia, council members enjoyed a block of seats, probably towards the front of the audience (cf. *Peace* 715, 905; *Birds* 794) and the same may have happened at the Lenaea. The humour of Agorakritos' narrative will have been heightened in performance if he spoke from the front of the *orkhēstra*, close to the council members, ribbing them in the eyes of the rest of the audience as he satirizes the way the council's business is conducted – he might even address the councillors in the audience with the direct speech contained in his narrative (642–5, 654–6).

The councillors at once lost interest in Paphlagon's accusations of a conspiracy and were ready to crown Agorakritos for bringing good news (646–7). This is a significant moment. In classical Athens, wearing a crown was a sign of celebration, or victory (e.g. in poetic competition or sport), or religious or political function, however temporary: in the political realm, holders of public office and citizens addressing the assembly wore crowns. Agorakritos proves himself worthy of a crown several times in the play (221, 646–7, 1250): Demosthenes tells him to crown himself when he is ready to face Paphlagon; the council are ready to crown Agorakritos for his news about the sardines; and at his final victory (1227–8, cf. 1250), Demos bestows Paphlagon's crown on him. The word for 'good news' (Gk. *euaggelia*) implicitly used by the council (647) is a humorous exaggeration, since to sacrifice in celebration of *euaggelia* was a civic or military act of great significance, appropriate for an important victory (Xenophon, *Hellenica* 4.3.14; Isocrates 7.10; Aeschines 3.160).

Next, Agorakritos tells the chorus that he advised the councillors to seize all the bowls from the craftsmen's shops, apparently so that they would have something hold to the sardines (cf. *Birds* 77). This plan was presented in secret (Gk. *aporrhēton*), like politically sensitive council business (cf. *Women at the Assembly* 442–4), a humorously self-defeating statement, since Agorakritos here reveals it to the chorus and the spectators. He continues to relate how the councillors clapped and stared at him, open-mouthed with stupefaction (651). 'Gaping' is a favourite image in Aristophanes, connoting simple-mindedness, astonishment, greed and loud, raucous speech, among other things; it is widely found in his plays, especially in *Cavalry* (see below).

Paphlagon tried to regain the council's favour by proposing a sacrifice of one hundred oxen (known as a 'hecatomb') to Athene (654–6). They swung his way until Agorakritos, seeing he was being overwhelmed by Paphlagon's 'cow dung' (658), proposed two hundred oxen to Athene and a vow on the next day to Artemis of 1,000 goats if pilchards sold for a hundred to the obol (658–62). Overmatched, Agorakritos says, Paphlagon started jabbering, so the presiding officials and the Scythian archers (security guards) started to haul him away (664–5).

Making outrageous promises is another kind of demagogic strategy – according to Thucydides (4.28.4), one that had propelled Cleon into command in the Pylos campaign. The public sacrifices that Paphlagon and Agorakritos propose would, if performed, benefit the city at large with copious handouts of meat, in quantities and value entirely disproportionate to the catch of fresh fish that they celebrate – the illogicality is the source of some of the humour. The numbers of animals promised for sacrifice here are exorbitant. In Athens, a hecatomb of oxen was sacrificed once a year at the Panathenaea festival, but on other occasions it was highly unusual to sacrifice so many: frequently, a sacrifice of a 'hecatomb' did not actually amount to the one hundred animals that its name implied. After Conon's victory in the battle of Cnidus in 393 BCE, the Athenians sacrificed 'an *actual* hecatomb' in celebration of this singular victory (Athenaeus 1.3d). The sacrifice of a thousand goats proposed by Agorakritos is meant to be yet more outrageous. In 490 BCE, before the battle of Marathon, the Athenians vowed to sacrifice 500 goats to Artemis every year if they were victorious over the Persians, so a proposal of 1,000 goats suggests the news about the sardines is twice as significant. Agorakritos' victory over Paphlagon with promises of gigantic public feasts prefigures the way in which he will defeat Paphlagon with gifts of food in their final contest (Chapter 7).

In a last-ditch attempt to regain the initiative, Agorakritos says, Paphlagon urged the council to wait to listen to a herald from Sparta proposing peace (a desperate and hypocritical strategy in view of Cleon's bellicose policies: cf. 794–6). But the councillors were now happy to let the war continue, so long as sardines were selling at a good price (667–73); they ended the session, leapt over the railings to leave the council chamber, and went to the marketplace, a satirical description of indecorous behaviour that emphasizes their self-interest and greed (674–5). Agorakritos closes his narrative by telling the chorus how he cemented his victory: he ran ahead of the councillors and bought up all the coriander and onions in the market, giving them away gratis to the overjoyed cheers of the council (676–82). In this way, he says, he has returned from the contest having won over the council with 'an obol of coriander' (681–2). The cheap price at which the councillors have been bought closes Agorakritos' satire on the workings of the council, who are more concerned about food and public celebrations than conspiracies or peace treaties.

With the narrative of offstage action complete, the chorus praises Agorakritos for outdoing Paphlagon in every sort of crime, mendacity and flattery (683–7). Their praise of his 'wily words' (687) uses a rare term for cunning (Gk. *haimulos*), otherwise only found once in Aristophanes (*Lysistrata* 1269), indicating Agorakritos' supreme powers of dissembling. Next, the chorus warn Agorakritos to consider how he may best prepare for more contesting (688–9; Gk. *agōniei*), a metatheatrical nod to the next sequence of stage action, the second agon. The remainder of the episode, before the second agon begins, restages many of the play's motifs. Paphlagon and Agorakritos compete to outdo one another in swearing oaths (e.g. 694–5), making threats (e.g. 705, 708–11) and accusations (e.g. 716–18) and hurling insults (e.g. 706–7, 721). It is noticeable here that Agorakritos is beginning to enjoy the battle (696–7), in contrast to his initial terror at the first sight of Paphlagon (240–1).

One of these exchanges deserves special mention. At 702, Paphlagon swears an oath by the 'front-row seats' (Gk. *prohedria*) he won at Pylos – one of numerous allusions to the privileges conferred on Cleon after his victory there (cf. 709). This privilege of 'VIP seating' will have placed Cleon at the front of the audience of *Cavalry* (cf. 203). Agorakritos' response (703–4), that he is looking forward to seeing Paphlagon in the back of the audience, could be directed at Cleon himself – no doubt, to the entertainment of many spectators sitting behind him – and would imply his removal from the focus of politics to a passive spectator (Slater 2002: 77).

Paphlagon, after an arrogant boast that he controls the democratic assembly (719–20), suggests that they call on the old man Demos, to decide their contest (723). Agorakritos agrees. The way that Paphlagon calls Demos out of his house develops a theme that has only been hinted at before this point (cf. 351–2): the erotic language with which politicians declare their love (Gk. *erōs*) for the demos. Here, Paphlagon addresses Demos as 'dearest little Demos' – an affectionate and highly familiar diminutive (726). In reply, Demos, as he comes out of the house, asks 'Who, Paphlagon, does you wrong?' (730), echoing some verses of the Greek poet Sappho, who was famous for her love poetry: 'Who, Sappho, does you wrong?' (Sappho, fr. 1.19-20 Campbell; cf. Kugelmeier 1996: 158–9).

The erotic political rhetoric in *Cavalry* is not simply a comic image of the lengths to which politicians must go to win the favour of the people. It was a real-life feature of Athenian political discourse, possibly one used by Cleon himself (cf. Connor 1971: 97–102; Wohl 2002: 92–3).[3] In Thucydides' description of the first public funeral of the Peloponnesian war (2.43.1), Pericles urges every Athenian to become a 'lover of the city' (Gk. *erastēs tēs poleōs*). Just how commonplace erotic rhetoric was in late fifth-century Athens is shown by further jokes in Aristophanes (*Acharnians* 143; *Birds* 1279) and other evidence: by the time the Platonic dialogues were being written, in the fourth century, being a 'lover of the Athenian demos' has become an ironic metaphor for pursuing a political career (Plato, *Gorgias* 481d; [Plato] *Alcibiades* I.132a). Therefore, when Paphlagon is said to have silenced the Athenians by 'making out with the

polis' (351–2), and later when Agorakritos confronts a rejuvenated
Demos with his former gullible behaviour ('in the assembly, when a
speaker said "Demos, I am your lover …"': 1340–1), the point is satirical
rather than purely absurd (see Wohl 2002: 73–123).

Yet there is absurdity to be found in Aristophanes' portrayal of erotic
political rhetoric. It is expressed by figuring Paphlagon and Agorakritos
as participants in a pederastic rivalry for the affections of Demos.
Homoerotic (i.e. same gender) pederasty (literally, 'sexual desire for a
youth') was a feature of ancient Greek culture from at least the seventh
century on. There is no clear evidence of it in Hesiod and Homer, but it
begins to appear in the poetry of the seventh and sixth centuries and in
vase painting from the same period on. It was practised by both men
and women. Female homoerotic pederasty is a central theme of the
poetry of Sappho and is found in vase-painting. The male form is
documented in a plethora of sources, including lyric poetry, comedy,
oratory, philosophy, history, vase-painting and graffiti (Hubbard 2003).

In late fifth-century Athens, male homoerotic pederasty was probably
seen as a relic of aristocratic culture (*Cavalry* 1387; cf. *Clouds* 961–83)
and depictions of it in surviving Athenian pottery decline from before
the middle of the century (Dover 1978: 7). Nevertheless, it is clear that
the practice continued throughout and far beyond the classical period. It
seems to be predominantly a feature of elite culture (cf. *Cavalry* 738),
though the nature of the evidence, which was largely produced by or for
elites, no doubt clouds the picture. In Aristophanic comedy, which had
to appeal to an audience from across the social spectrum and therefore
probably one weighted towards non-elites, pederasty is the source of
plenty of humour (e.g. *Cavalry* 736–40, *Birds* 137–42, *Wealth* 153–9).

At its core, male homoerotic pederasty in ancient Greece was the
ritualized courtship of an adolescent or young man by an older
adolescent or adult male. In Greek, the older 'lover' was known as the
erastēs, the younger as the 'beloved' or *erōmenos*. Successful courtship
would lead to certain forms of sexual interaction (Dover 1978: 91–100).
It is generally believed that whatever happened usually stopped short of
penetrative sex, which could expose the *erōmenos* to the charge of

prostitution and potential loss of citizenship. Though consent could be encouraged by gifts, sexual activity was not supposed to involve payment. It is generally held that the culmination of these relationships was intercrural sex (i.e. with the *erōmenos* allowing the *erastēs*' penis between his thighs for stimulation). However, neither the visual evidence of painted pottery nor the written record of ancient texts clearly sets out exactly what was done or how or when.[4]

To illustrate, a sixth-century black-figure amphora (Figure 4) depicts some of the practices of courtship and sexual activity. A young man, identified by the absence of a beard, stands surrounded by numerous older men bringing hunting dogs and fighting cocks as love gifts (the latter were often connected with hunting, sport, or music: cf. Dover 1978: 92). The two men nearest the youth touch him: the one standing behind him touches his buttocks; the one in front fondles his (flaccid) penis and touches his cheek, gazing closely at his face, perhaps looking for a kiss. From other evidence, it is known, for example, that the wrestling ground was a place where boys might be approached, and the gifts they received were not necessarily material: the fourth-century politician Aeschines (1.135), who says he has been in love with many boys, admits to having written erotic poetry for them.

The ongoing joke in *Cavalry* is that Paphlagon and Agorakritos turn the practice of pederasty upside down, another of the play's many images of inversion. They express erotic desire for Demos, a decrepit old man (cf. 42–4, 752 etc.), and seek his favour with protestations of love and courtship gifts. Paphlagon calls himself Demos' *erastēs* (732), and Agorakritos introduces himself as an *anterastēs*, a rival lover (733), followed by a complaint that the old man is drawn to the wrong sort of wooers, tradesmen like Paphlagon rather than the wellborn and upstanding (736–40); the irony of Agorakritos' words here, given his profession, is palpable. The theme of pederasty is concentrated in the first half of the next episode, the second agon, but it runs through the second half of the play (cf. 1162–3).

The principal difference between Paphlagon and a 'noble' lover, who offers wisdom, guidance and love gifts, is that Paphlagon gives Demos

money (contrary to the idealized practices of pederasty: cf. *Wealth* 155–
6), especially in the form of pay for jury service (cf. 945 where Demos
characterizes the people as the 'many-an-obol'), which suggests
symbolically that Demos is perilously close to becoming a prostitute
(Gk. *pornos*) to his demagogues (Bennett and Tyrell 1990: 242–4; Wohl
2002: 86–7). Payment for civic service is heavily thematized in *Cavalry*.
Jury-pay (the 'triobolon') is only associated with Paphlagon (51, 255,
800), who also offers Demos pay for nothing (905) and predicts future
pay through oracles (798, 1019). Agorakritos never offers Demos jury-
pay, though he promises to remit payment for military service (1079).
He accuses Paphlagon of misusing state pay (804) and Demos of
habitually voting for it in preference to better uses of the revenue of the
empire (1352–3). After his rejuvenation, Demos promises to pay rowers
on time (1367).

At the close of the episode, Paphlagon persuades Demos to judge
between them in the assembly (746). This will be a competition to
decide who is more 'well-minded' (Gk. *eunous*) towards the people
(748), a theme developed in the next episode. Agorakritos agrees to an
assembly but begs Demos not to hold it on the Pnyx, the low hill to the
west of the acropolis where most assemblies were held (749; for a map,
see Figure 1). But Demos will not be persuaded to abandon his
customary seat (750–1). The staging is uncertain, but the old man
might sit on a low rock in the *orkhēstra* (754; cf. Slater 2002: 77),
symbolizing an assembly held on the Pnyx. There, as Agorakritos
exclaims in horror, Demos loses his habitual intelligence and becomes
a gaping-mouthed fool (752–5).

The word (Gk.) *khaskein*, meaning 'gape' or 'open the mouth wide', is
often found in Aristophanes. Evidently, ancient Greeks thought the
action unsophisticated and undignified (cf. *Birds* 165–6). Since the
comic mask has a large opening for a mouth, it will have been easy for
actors to perform the gesture, which has various connotations. The
most common in Aristophanes are stupidity, astonishment, shock,
helplessness, and so on (e.g. *Cavalry* 261, 651, 755, 1032, 1119, 1263; cf.
Acharnians 133; *Frogs* 990). The gesture also indicates greed or desire

for things such as entertainment, food, sex, or wine (e.g. *Acharnians* 10; *Cavalry* 804; *Clouds* 996; *Lysistrata* 426), and loud and undignified speech (e.g. *Cavalry* 956; *Peace* 57). The word is found more often in *Cavalry* than other plays and repeatedly characterizes Demos, the council, and the city as stupid, greedy, and in thrall to their demagogues.[5]

Second agon (756–941)

In some plays of Aristophanes (*Cavalry, Clouds, Wasps, Birds*), the central issue of the plot is not resolved in a single agon, and the play incorporates a second one. The second agon in *Cavalry* follows the pattern of the first: each section is introduced by a strophic choral ode, in the usual way, but instead of speeches, there are two dialogues between Paphlagon and Agorakritos, with the latter emerging victorious at the end of each (821–2, 946–8). The topic of the second agon is demagogic 'love' for the Athenian people.

The strophe (756–60), like the antistrophe that answers it, alludes to *Prometheus Bound* (usually attributed to Aeschylus). The chorus' description (759) of Paphlagon as 'resourceful at scheming schemes even when without resource' echoes *Prometheus Bound* (59 and perhaps also 308), the implication being that Paphlagon is an adversary as formidable and cunning as the titan Prometheus who stole fire from the gods to give it to humanity.[6]

Paphlagon speaks first, an indication that he will be the loser in the agon (see Chapter 4). He begins with a prayer, as meetings of the assembly did, and a self-curse (763–8):

Paphlagon   To lady Athene, ruler of the city, I utter my prayer
that if I have been towards the demos of Athens the best of men,
after Lysikles, Kynna, and Salabakkho, may I dine in the Prytaneion,
even as I do now, for having done nothing.
But if I hate you, Demos, and do not singlehandedly go forth to do
    battle for you,
may I die and be sawn in two and cut up into leather yoke-straps.

The oracle read in the prologue alluded to Lysikles (132) as the demagogue immediately preceding Paphlagon. Kynna and Salabakkho were two famous prostitutes, as mentions of them elsewhere in Aristophanes show (cf. *Wasps* 1032; *Peace* 755; *Women at the Thesmophoria* 805); their sexual services to the Athenian people, the prayer implies, have been of more use than Paphlagon's leadership. The reference to dining in the Prytaneion evokes Cleon's singular reward for the Pylos campaign, where Paphlagon admits that he did nothing. The absurdly self-condemnatory proclamations of Paphlagon's prayer indicate, like his being first to speak, that this is another contest he will lose.

Agorakritos trumps Paphlagon with a more violent self-curse drawn from his trade of butchery: 'may I be cut up *and* boiled in little chunks' (769–70). The phrase 'if I do not love you and cherish you ...' (769) in Agorakritos' curse uses the word (Gk.) *stergein* ('cherish'), which is rare in Aristophanes and is not found in passages of ordinary speech (cf. *Wasps* 1054; *Frogs* 229; *Women at the Assembly* 291, 897). The elevated poetic diction anticipates Agorakritos' proof of greater love for Demos than Paphlagon. Paphlagon, by contrast, mostly uses the general term for 'love' (Gk.) *philein* (773, 791, 821), which is extremely common in Aristophanes; but he betrays the cynicism behind his protestations of love by describing the contest as one in 'flattery'.

Here, Aristophanes' word for 'flattery' is significant: (Gk.) *thōpeumatia* (788) is found nowhere else and is perhaps an Aristophanic coinage, while (Gk.) *thōpeia* (890) is seldom found in ancient Greek and in Aristophanes appears only here. The unusual vocabulary develops the theme of flattery found in the prologue (48; cf. Edwards 2010: 323), with these rare words emphasizing Paphlagon's political tactics: he 'sucks up' to Demos rather than sincerely caring for him. Another aspect of Paphlagon's characterization that prefigures his defeat is worth mentioning: his status as a slave would disqualify him, in Athenian law, from having an *erōmenos*; the penalty for a slave who so much as followed a boy was fifty lashes (Aeschines 1.139).

But actions, not words, win the contest. After Paphlagon claims his love for Demos has been demonstrated by his many prosecutions,

which benefited him as well as the public (773–6), Agorakritos replies
by giving the old man a cushion to sit on (784–5) – so that the victor of
the battle of Marathon will not chafe the backside that once sat on a
trireme's bench at the battle of Salamis (781, 785). Agorakritos' words
evoke Athens' 'golden age', in the Persian Wars, now more than fifty
years ago: the effect is to contrast the degradation of the democracy
under Cleon's leadership with the 'good old days', when Athens saved
Greece from Persia. Notably, Paphlagon does not give Demos anything
other than words. On stage, the contrast between the two rivals for
Demos' love will have been made clear when Agorakritos produces a
cushion and places it for Demos to sit on – an eye-catching piece of
stage action with the use of a new prop. The old man asks Agorakritos
(786) if he is descended from the tyrannicide Harmodios. This would
be pointedly irritating to Cleon, especially if he had boasted of a family
connexion to Harmodios (see Chapter 4). Since the closest descendants
of the tyrannicides were eligible to dine in the Prytaneion (cf. *IG* i^3
131.5-7), Demos' question might suggest that Agorakritos is worthy of
an honour that Paphlagon has achieved but does not deserve (573–6).
Moreover, Demos describes Agorakritos' gift as (Gk.) *philodēmon*,
'showing love for the demos', anticipating his victory in the agon.

Again, Paphlagon proclaims his love for Demos in words (791), but
Agorakritos is ready with a rebuttal. He points out that many Athenians
have been living in shacks in the city for seven years, since the evacuation
of Attica at the beginning of the war – a war that Paphlagon has only
prolonged (792–6), using the emergency to conceal his many crimes
(801–4). The accusation here is very similar to an assessment of Cleon's
policy of continuing the war found in Thucydides (5.16.1): 'Cleon
thought that if peace came, his crimes would be more easily noticed,
and his smears less persuasive.'

One of Paphlagon's tactics of obfuscation is reciting oracles (cf. 61).
Here, he claims that an oracle predicts that Demos will go to court in
Arcadia, earning five obols for jury service, up from the present three
obols (797–9). Since Arcadia is in the mountains of the central
Peloponnese, the implication is that Athens will not only defeat Sparta

but conquer the Peloponnesians entirely – a remote prospect to say the least. In the meantime, Paphlagon says, he will feed and care for (Gk. *therapeuein*) Demos with his three obols a day (799–800). Paphlagon's use of (Gk.) *therapeuein* is the only word other than (Gk.) *philein* that he uses to express love for Demos, but the public-spiritedness it implies is undercut when Paphlagon adds that he will give Demos his three obols 'by fair means or foul'.

Paphlagon's final attempt to show democratic spirit in the first half of the agon is a ridiculous boast. He claims to have done more for Athens than Themistocles (810–12). Among other achievements, Themistocles was the architect of the Athenian fleet, the harbour in Piraeus (cf. 815, 885) and the extension of Athens' walls (Thucydides 1.93.2), as well as the victor of the battle of Salamis in 480 BCE.[7] The ludicrousness of Paphlagon's boast is reflected in Agorakritos' reaction: he quotes from Euripides' *Telephus* (fr. 713 Collard-Cropp), 'O city of Argos, do you hear how he talks?' This expression, deriving from a tragedy performed nearly fifteen years before *Cavalry*, must have become a popular catchphrase in Athens, used as an exclamation of astonished disbelief; Aristophanes is still using it over thirty-five years later (*Wealth* 601).

Paphlagon declares his love for Demos once more (820–1); but this time his empty words are rejected, and Demos remarks that he has been aware for a long time that Paphlagon has been bamboozling him (821–2; cf. 1121–30, 1141–50 for Demos' concealed awareness of political corruption). The word for 'bamboozling' (Gk.) *egkruphiazein* (822) is extremely rare – it occurs only here in classical Greek – and probably is used to emphasize Paphlagon's extraordinary talent for political obfuscation. Demos' affection for Paphlagon, made clear a short time ago (730), has been reversed. Now, Agorakritos addresses Demos with an even more unusual and exaggerated diminutive ('my darlingest little Demos', 823) than Paphlagon used earlier (726), signalling that he has gained the upper hand in the contest to be the more devoted lover of Demos.

The first half of the agon ends with another fast-paced exchange of accusations and threats (824–34). Agorakritos accuses Paphlagon of embezzlement and accepting bribes from the allies (824–7, 832–4) and is threatened with an enormous lawsuit (828–9). Agorakritos' accusation that Paphlagon has accepted a bribe from Mytilene may have had special satirical bite if a detail of Thucydides' record of Cleon's words in the assembly is historically precise. According to Thucydides (3.38.2), Cleon had suggested, barely three years earlier, in an assembly debate over the fate of Mytilene that anyone who spoke in defence of the Mytileneans must have been bribed by them.[8] If the audience recalled this as a notably cynical argument, Agorakritos' accusation would turn a memorable attempt to prejudice the assembly against its author.

The second part of the 'love contest' opens with the chorus, in their antistrophe, congratulating and encouraging Agorakritos (836–40); the laudatory expression, 'You who have arisen as the greatest help for all people' (836), alludes, once more, to *Prometheus Bound* (613), suggesting that, by facing up to Paphlagon, Agorakritos has become like the titan Prometheus. The reversal of roles from the strophe, where Paphlagon was likened to Prometheus, highlights Agorakritos' progress towards victory.

Paphlagon begins the second half of the agon by boasting of his victory at Pylos (844–6), which had been commemorated with the public display of the shields taken from the captured Peloponnesians.[9] But this time he is defeated by one of his own tactics – making accusations of a plot against the democracy. Here, Agorakritos accuses Paphlagon of keeping the shields from Pylos ready for use in a revolution (847–57). In reply, Paphlagon declares himself the only man who can stop conspiracies against democracy (860–3), on the face of it an impressive claim, but in fact one that was wearily familiar in Athens (cf. [Demosthenes] 25.64). Agorakritos responds with a simile (Paphlagon stirs up confusion in Athens like an eel-fisher stirring up mud) and a gift to Demos of a pair of shoes (871–2) – pointedly a present of a kind that Paphlagon, as a 'leather monger', could have made had he wanted to (cf. 315–21).

The eel-fishing simile (one that Aristophanes was very proud of and later claimed that other comic poets had copied: *Clouds* 559) is part of the important theme of 'upheaval', 'disturbance' and 'confusion' in *Cavalry*. Agorakritos' words here are the fullest elaboration (864–7):

> **Agorakritos** You're just like the eel-catchers. When the lake is still, they catch nothing. But if they churn the mud up and down, they make a catch. And you, too, get something by stirring up the city!

The word most associated with this imagery is (Gk.) *tarattein* ('to stir up') and it is very prominent in the play; in fact, *tarattein* and compounds cognate with it occur considerably more frequently in *Cavalry* (66, 214, 247, 251, 309, 358, 431, 692, 840, 867, 902) than in any other play of Aristophanes (Edmunds 1987b: 234). Closely associated with *tarattein* is the word *kukan*, which shares the same basic meaning and, among Aristophanes' plays, is found most often in *Cavalry* (251, 363, 692, 866, 1286).

Elsewhere in Aristophanes, *tarattein* is used to describe mental confusion (*Acharnians* 688), acute psychological disturbance (*Wasps* 696) and gastric roiling (*Clouds* 386, 388); but most often it is a metaphor for political upheaval, especially that caused by war (*Acharnians* 621; *Peace* 266, 320; *Lysistrata* 565, 567). In *Cavalry*, the imagery of 'disturbance' and 'confusion' is used especially of Cleon's political activity (66, 431, 692, 867): even after Cleon's death, Aristophanes continues to associate the words *tarattein* and *kukan* with him (*Peace* 269–70, 313–20). Frequently, the imagery of disturbance figures Cleon as a storm threatening the ship of state (Edmunds 1987a.14-15, 1987b.233-47). In *Wasps* (1285), Aristophanes uses a compound form of the verb (Gk. *hypotarattein*) to describe how Cleon harassed him in the law-courts. Throwing Athens – and Paphlagon himself – into confusion is what Agorakritos must learn to do to become the Athenians' worst demagogue yet (cf. 214–15, 251, 358, 840). It is a feature of the second agon that, in the last use of *tarattein* in the play, Paphlagon admits himself 'confounded' – and therefore defeated – by Agorakritos' jokes (902).

Agorakritos' gift of a pair of shoes for Demos is the first of a series of significant stage-actions. At every point in the second half of this agon, Agorakritos will give Demos a gift (four in total), while Paphlagon, with one exception, will offer only empty words. As in the first part of the agon, when Agorakritos gave Demos a cushion to sit on, his repeated action of gift-giving will have had a visual impact on the audience beyond the impression that the text makes on the reader.

Here, Agorakritos' victory is marked by the culmination of the motif of being (Gk.) *eunous*, 'well-minded', or 'having goodwill', toward the people. Earlier (748) Paphlagon had identified 'goodwill' as the decisive factor in the second agon; since then, Agorakritos has accused Paphlagon of lacking 'well-mindedness' (779), Paphlagon has been infuriated that Agorakritos is coming to seem 'well-minded' through 'little flatteries' (788), and finally, with the gift of the shoes, Demos has judged Agorakritos, with a humorous paraprosdokian, 'most well-minded to me and my toes' (874). It is notable that the only other appearance of *eunous* in the play (690) is a declaration of the chorus's support for Agorakritos; in short, Paphlagon is never seen to be 'well-minded' in any way, and Aristophanes' choice of words is a fine piece of characterization that prefigures Paphlagon's defeat in the second agon and in the play overall. It is worth remarking that the emotional intensity of 'goodwill', (Gk.) *eunoia*, is less even than 'friendship' or 'affection' (Aristotle, *Nicomachean Ethics* 1166b30-4; Scholtz 2004: 270); the implication is that Paphlagon's rhetoric of love is insincere: he sets the competition up over something that falls short of love and then fails even to demonstrate that.

Without a gift for Demos, Paphlagon says that he has something better: he has expelled a man called Grypos from civic life by convicting him of prostituting himself (877). The latter was a serious offence for a citizen in classical Athens and if proved resulted in loss of citizen privileges: there is a famous example of just such a prosecution in Aeschines' speech *Against Timarchus*, from 346/5 BCE (Aeschines 1.19-20, cf. 29). Again, Agorakritos responds with a gift, after humorously suggesting that the only reason Paphlagon is interested in prosecuting male prostitutes is to prevent them from becoming politicians – a favourite Aristophanic joke (cf. 425-8; *Assembly Women* 112-13).

This time, Agorakritos' gift is a tunic that fits over both shoulders for added warmth in winter (881-3). Since the Lenaea was held in the late winter, the action may have been reinforced if Demos' costume left him somewhat underdressed for the season. The stage business of Demos putting on the tunic must have required a pause in the actors' speech (it would have to be pulled over the actor's mask or fastened around his shoulders), again highlighting the importance, here, of Agorakritos' gifts in a way that the text alone cannot make fully clear.

At this point, Agorakritos has dressed Demos with a new tunic and sandals – a powerful visual symbol of his progress towards political primacy. There is a parallel at the end of the play when Demos appears not just rejuvenated but once more reclothed (cf. 1331). Demos thanks Agorakritos by saying that his gift has outdone even Themistocles' construction of the harbour in Piraeus (884). The exaggerated compliment acquires extra potency because Paphlagon has very recently claimed to have benefitted the city more than Themistocles (811–12).

Paphlagon tries to compete with Agorakritos by dressing Demos up further (891), possibly with a cloak, but the text does not make clear what the garment is (perhaps an apron or a belt if Cleon was known for wearing one: see Chapter 2). But the old man is disgusted by the stench of leather and rejects the gesture, telling Paphlagon to 'go to the crows' (i.e. 'fuck off and die': 890–2). Agorakritos, taking his cue from the stench, accuses Paphlagon of having plotted to cause juries to suffocate themselves with their own flatulence by providing them with cheap silphium, a highly prized (and now extinct) vegetable (893–901, cf. 847–57).[10]

Agorakritos is beginning to beat Paphlagon at his habitual games. As he explains, he is merely adopting Paphlagon's methods to defeat him, like a man borrowing someone else's slippers to go out into the street to defecate (888–9). Paphlagon continues to offer Demos nothing but empty words (904–5, 908): he promises future benefits and attentions but gives the old man nothing. Agorakritos once more trumps him with gifts: ointment for Demos' leg-sores (906–7) and a soft hare's tail to wipe his eyes with (909).

The second agon closes with a pnigos, this time a rapid volley of threats from Paphlagon, parried by inventive and humorous replies from Agorakritos. Paphlagon threatens to ruin Agorakritos financially by burdening him with maintaining a decrepit trireme and crushing him with emergency wartime taxes (912–18, 923–6).[11] The trierarchy and the (Gk.) *eisphora* were heavy contributions to the polis that fell only on the wealthiest Athenians. Note that even the threat of them suggests Agorakritos' rise from lowly sausage-seller to the company of the wealthy elite. In response, Agorakritos makes a joke about the symbolism of Paphlagon's name (919: 'bubbler', see Chapter 3), and utters a prayer that Paphlagon will choke on a piece of squid and lose a bribe by missing the assembly (927–40).

Agorakritos' closing prayer mirrors Paphlagon's prayer (763–8), with which the agon began: the 'book-ending' of the agon with two prayers is an example of the poetic technique of ring composition. Furthermore, this prayer, pronounced in a run of short lines (927–40), is one of the longest sequences performed by an actor in the pnigos (see Chapter 3) of any agon in Aristophanes (cf. *Clouds* 1009–23; *Women at the Assembly* 689–709). If it was spoken in a single breath, it probably will have impressed the audience as a virtuoso piece of skill. That Aristophanes designed this 'choker' as a showpiece is suggested also by a metatheatrical joke in the very last word (Gk. *epapopnigesthai*) of Agorakritos' prayer, where the pnigos comes to an end: Agorakritos says 'may you choke!' (640).[12]

As is conventional in an agon, the chorus close with their verdict, implied by their joyful invocation of the gods: Agorakritos has won (941). His victory has been achieved by giving Demos gifts – five in total – while the only gift that Paphlagon offered was rejected (891–2). The contrast between Agorakritos' generosity and Paphlagon's calculated self-interest will reappear in a decisive role in the final contest (Chapter 7).

Episode (942–72)

Agorakritos has emerged victorious in the second agon. In the short episode that follows, Demos has decided that he is fed up with Paphlagon's talk of loving him (946). He orders Paphlagon to return his signet-ring so that he can give it to Agorakritos, removing Paphlagon from his office as custodian of Athens. Paphlagon gives Demos the ring he is wearing (948–50), predicting that if Demos does not allow him to oversee matters, a more villainous man than he will appear – this evokes, again, the motif of a demagogic succession established in the oracle in the prologue and once more misdirects the audience about the surprise denouement of the play. In the second agon (see above), Agorakritos has given Demos five gifts, all gratefully accepted. Soon, he will receive one in return (959). In the meantime, Demos demands that Paphlagon return a gift, the ring, that he once gave him (947–8), symbolizing Paphlagon's failure in the contest for Demos' affections.

It turns out that the ring Paphlagon returns is not Demos' but Cleonymus' (958). Cleonymus was a prominent political ally of Cleon. He is repeatedly ridiculed by Aristophanes as obese (e.g. *Acharnians* 88), a glutton (e.g. *Birds* 289) and a coward (e.g. *Clouds* 353–4). Since Cleon was at the time the most influential man in Athens, there is humour in the implication that Paphlagon is really Cleonymus' subordinate. The symbolic point is even clearer: according to Demos, Paphlagon did not have his ring at all; therefore, his leadership of the people has never been legitimate. Demos gives Agorakritos the proper ring (959), presumably from his own hand – another eye-catching piece of stage action.

Paphlagon begs Demos to wait until he has listened to a collection of oracles before making Agorakritos his favoured leader. This sets the scene for the next contest: persuasion of the assembly with oracular predictions (Chapter 6). Agorakritos replies that he too will bring forth oracles (960–72). Each contestant threatens terrible consequences if the other's oracles are believed (962–3, 963–4) and promises glorious predictions from their own (965–6, 967–9).

It is of note that while the oracles Agorakritos says he will recite are clearly outrageous comic parody of the oracles that Paphlagon has promised (963–4, 967–9), Paphlagon's oracles have a ring of authenticity. His second oracle predicts that Athens will rule the world and be crowned with roses (965–6); though it cannot be linked to any known oracle text, the tone of it is not obviously humorous or parodic, and some genuine oracular text may lie behind it. Moreover, the first oracle Paphlagon mentions is certainly historical (Aristophanes alludes to it more than once, so it was clearly well-known in fifth-century Athens): the mention of a 'leather bottle' (963) evokes an image of Athenian resilience found in a Delphic oracle known from Plutarch (*Life of Theseus* 24.5); the final lines urge the Athenians to be of good heart, 'for a bottle in the waves will cross the sea'. Plutarch also records that the Sibyl (a prophetess) restated the oracle with the verse: 'A bottle may be submerged but remember that it cannot sink.' If Cleon was known for quoting oracles in the assembly (cf. 61), Paphlagon's reliance here on well-known oracular predictions about Athens will be satirical rather than absurd.

Aristophanes takes the opportunity here to ridicule Cleon's tannery once more. The word Paphlagon uses for 'bottle' is not the word used in the oracle quoted by Plutarch, which is (Gk.) *askos*, meaning a bladder made of animal hide. Instead, Paphlagon uses a vulgar Thracian word (cf. Beekes *s.v.*), (Gk.) *molgos*, meaning a bottle made of leather. This seems to have been a well-known and deliberately humorous misquotation of the oracle, for Aristophanes uses it more than once (frr. 103, 308, 933 Henderson). Here, it has special resonance because it plays on Paphlagon's characterization as a foreigner and a slave who follows a despised trade – suggesting, naturally, that these are all features of Cleon.

Ode (973–96)

Paphlagon and Agorakritos leave the stage to collect their stashes of oracles, and the chorus sing before the next contest begins. Their song is a short strophic ode attacking Cleon – his name appears for the only time in the play (976). Aristophanes' intention in naming Cleon here may have been to popularize the song so that it would be sung independently of the play, perhaps as a drinking song (Gk. *skolion*) at symposiums (Slater 2002: 78 with n. 33; Parker 1997: 176 observes that its simple metre makes it likely that it was intended to be catchy).

In the strophe, the chorus sing of Cleon's most devoted supporters, the old men who enjoy pay for sitting on juries. Cleon is figured as a pair of kitchen utensils: a pestle and a spoon (984). Since these implements are used for pounding and stirring, the image is a variation on the theme of (Gk.) *tarattein* (discussed above). The idea of Cleon as a pestle is also found in *Peace* (269–70).

In the antistrophe, the chorus makes a joke of Cleon's education, which they call his 'pig-music' (cf. *Wasps* 36 for Cleon's voice being like that of an 'enraged sow'). Music (*mousikē*) was an essential part of advanced education in ancient Greece. The chorus sings that Cleon was expelled from school for accepting bribes, saying he would only tune his lyre to play in the 'bass-clef-tomaniac' (996). The suggestion that Cleon was a failure in music recalls Agorakritos' complete lack of musical education (191–3): insufficient musical training makes a man suitable for the trade of demagogue, but Agorakritos, with no training in music at all, is notably worse, as the oracle has predicted, than the man whom he will surpass to become leader of Athens.

6

Cavalry 997–1150: Divination Contest and Duet

After the second agon, the next contest between Agorakritos and Paphlagon is an episode called, here, the 'divination contest' (997–1110). In it Paphlagon and Agorakritos read (or pretend to read) oracles and describe prophetic dreams. They also offer interpretations of their oracles: that is to say, they employ the practice of divination. The oracles are a bricolage of comic parody and pastiche intended to flatter or otherwise manipulate Demos.

At the end of the divination contest, Demos much prefers Agorakritos' oracles, and Paphlagon is defeated once more. Before the next episode begins, the chorus and Demos sing a 'duet' (1111–50). The chorus accuses Demos of stupidity and gullibility, and the old man rebukes them: he only pretends not to notice what politicians are up to, so that he can enjoy the pay they dole out to buy his favour; he allows demagogues to rise so that he can take pleasure and profit in bringing them down.

Episode (997–1110)

Oracles are an essential ingredient of *Cavalry*: they structure the plot and appear as a significant theme. In the prologue, Demosthenes interprets an oracle to foretell that Agorakritos has been divinely chosen to rid Athens of Paphlagon (Chapter 3). After Agorakritos' final victory, Paphlagon questions his adversary and confirms his deepest fear: as an oracle has predicted, Agorakritos is indeed the man by whom he is destined to be vanquished (Chapter 7). Thus, *Cavalry* dramatizes the fulfilment of an oracle, a plot device familiar from tragedy.

The oracle stolen by Nicias in the prologue (109–45) is not the only one in *Cavalry*. Oracles (and prophetic dreams) are heavily thematized in the play. They are another means by which Paphlagon dupes the Athenians (61, 797–9, 809, 818). Note that until the 'divination contest', all the oracles and dreams mentioned in the play are Paphlagon's. Like the erotic rhetoric of the second agon (Chapter 5), divination, however strange it might seem now, was a real feature of Athenian political discourse.

Oracles, poetic texts of (supposedly) divine inspiration, were only one form of the practice of divination, which is the interpretation of signs from the gods. Other divinatory practices in ancient Greece included extispicy (inspection of the entrails of sacrificial victims), ornithomancy (observing the flight patterns and calls of birds) and oneiromancy (the interpretation of dreams). The social function of divination was to provide a means of deciding how to act in uncertain situations, where the risks (or the stakes in competing interests) were high and the chances of a successful (or acceptable) outcome either finely balanced or impossible to ascertain. For example, before joining Cyrus' rebellion against the Persian king Artaxerxes II, the mercenary solider Xenophon went to Delphi to ask Apollo what sacrifices he should make for a successful campaign (*Anabasis* 3.1.5-7).

The most famous oracles, like the 'wooden-wall' oracle given to the Athenians before the battle of Salamis (Herodotus 7.141), came from shrines of the gods, like that of Apollo at Delphi or Zeus at Dodona. They carried great authority in political matters (see e.g. Demosthenes 18.253, 19.297-9; Dinarchus 1.78, 98). Less well-known, but not necessarily less influential in political debate, were the prophecies of legendary seers like Bacis, whose oracles Paphlagon claims to recite in this episode. Such oracular predictions were collected in books owned by a 'chresmologue' (Gk. *khrēsmologos*), an 'oracle collector'; chresmologues would read out or quote oracles to their audiences and offer interpretation. In the 'divination contest', the role of the chresmologue is usurped and parodied by Paphlagon and Agorakritos.

The existence of books of oracles had long been a feature of ancient Greek life, not least in Athens. Herodotus' story (7.6.3-5) of the chresmologue Onomakritos is an illustration. In the late sixth century, Hipparchus, brother of Hippias, the last tyrant of Athens, banished Onomakritos, who had a collection of the oracles of the seer Musaeus. The reason for Onomakritos' banishment was an accusation that he had inserted a spurious oracle into the collection. Later, Onomakritos was reconciled with Hipparchus and joined him in exile at the court of Xerxes, where he began proclaiming oracles favourable to Persia. In short, the famous chresmologue Onomakritos was probably a forger and certainly a traitor and the flunky of any patron he could find. However, it would be wrong to draw the conclusion that chresmologues were always assumed to be unscrupulous and their oracles to be fakes: punishing a chresmologue for falsifying an oracle in his collection implies the need to preserve the integrity of an authentic book of oracles, as well as the authority of an accepted practice of divination.

Musaeus was only one among numerous legendary prophets whose inspired verses were recorded in books known in Aristophanes' day. Other collections mentioned in fifth-century sources are those of Bacis, Sibylla (the Sibyl of Erythrae), Orpheus and Laius, and it is probable, on the evidence of later sources, that there were many more.[1] But it is the oracles of Bacis that seem to have been the most influential in the fifth century. In his account of the Persian Wars, Herodotus refers to prophecies of Bacis and Musaeus at several points. Yet while he quotes Bacis' verses three times (Herodotus 8.20; 8.77, cf. 8.96.2; 9.43), he never records a word of Musaeus. Similarly, when Aristophanes ridicules chresmologues, though he mentions Sibylla, only Bacis is the source of quotations.

Aristophanes was fond of ridiculing chresmologues. In *Peace* (1052–1126) and *Birds* (959–91), a chresmologue interrupts the hero while he is making sacrifice and is driven from the stage. In *Peace*, the chresmologue is an historical individual, Hierokles of Oreos, a city in Euboea (cf. *Peace* 1046); some twenty years before *Cavalry*, he is found in an inscription in which he is appointed to head a delegation of three council members entrusted with making sacrifices ordained by an oracle (*IG* i³ 40.64-7). To the detriment of chresmologues, Aristophanes draws a clear distinction between oracles of ancient seers collected in books and oracles given by the gods, especially oracles of Apollo. The latter are treated with respect and are always held to be superior to the predictions of seers like Bacis and Sibylla. In *Cavalry*, oracles of Sybilla and Bacis are ruses for deceiving the Athenians (61, 1003), whereas the oracle that predicts Paphlagon's fall comes from Apollo. In *Birds* (981–2), Peisthetairos trumps the chresmologue's quotation of Bacis by claiming that he has an oracle from Apollo.

More damning still is Aristophanes' insinuation that chresmologues invent oracles after the events they appeared to foretell (*Peace* 1085; *Birds* 962–5). Mistrust of Bacis and Sybilla as sources of prophecy is evident in *Peace* and *Birds*. In *Peace*, Trygaios dismisses Sibylla as flat nonsense (1116, cf. 1095); in *Birds*, in a repeated gag, the chresmologue and Peisthetairos challenge each other to check what is written in their books (974, 980, 986, 989), implying that the authenticity of chresmologues' oracles is questionable.

In the early years of the Peloponnesian War, oracles about the plague were the subject of intense interest in Athens. Thucydides records several prophecies that were widely talked about at the outbreak of the war, two of them from Apollo's temple in Delphi. One of the Delphic oracles warned the Athenians against inhabiting the (Gk.) *pelargikon*, an empty plot of land in Athens, protected from habitation by a curse; when the war began, it was quickly occupied by refugees sheltering from the Peloponnesian invasion (Thucydides 2.17.1-2). Another oracle of Apollo prophesied that the Spartans would achieve victory if they fought with all their might and that Apollo himself would help them (Thucydides 1.118.3; cf. 1.123.1, 2.54.4). Since Apollo was the god of disease, both oracles seemed to come true with the outbreak of plague in Athens in 430.

But Delphi was not the only source of oracles about the plague. When the epidemic struck, Thucydides writes, the Athenians quoted a verse, which the older men 'said had long since been recited' (2.54.2): 'A Dorian war [i.e. one waged by Dorian-speaking Greeks like the Spartans] shall come and a sickness with it.' This vague prediction, which captured the imaginations of Athenians, seems to have been of unknown origin, and the true wording of it was the subject of dispute (Thucydides says that another version of it replaced 'sickness' with 'famine'). It was only one among many circulated at the time, and if it is representative of the kind of material promulgated by chresmologues, it is not hard to see why not everyone found their interventions helpful.

Before the outbreak of the war, Thucydides (2.8.2) writes, 'many prophecies were quoted, and many were chanted by chresmologues'. When the first invading Peloponnesian army advanced within sight of Athens' city walls, Thucydides describes the scene like this (2.21.3):

> [The Athenians] gathered in groups in heated debate, some urging a sortie, others resisting. Chresmologues were chanting oracles of all kinds, depending on how men were disposed to hear them.

One of these oracles was surely the prediction that Thucydides says he remembers from the beginning of the war that the conflict would last 'thrice nine years' (5.26.4). And no doubt there were oracles of Bacis among those chanted by the chresmologues. It is worth drawing attention to what this passage implies – the persuasive power of oracles in political debate, the tendency of individuals to listen to the oracles they wanted to hear, and the suspicious facility of the chresmologue to recite verses tailored to his audience. Each of these features of the political use of oracle books in Athens was a ready target for Aristophanic satire, and all appear in the divination contest in *Cavalry*.

The influence that oracles could hold over democratic debate in Athens should not be underestimated. It is illustrated by what Thucydides says about the disaster in Sicily in 413: when their forces were destroyed, the Athenians became enraged at the chresmologues and anyone else who had used divination to encourage the expedition (Thucydides 8.1.1). To be clear, this and other criticisms of divination found in Thucydides (e.g. 2.54.3; cf. 2.47.4, 5.26.3, 5.103.2, 7.50.4) are not necessarily indicative of disbelief in divination in general, merely of scepticism about the competence of many who claimed to be skilled practitioners and the undue influence they wielded. Similarly, the appearance of chresmologues and their oracles in Aristophanes is not 'cheap-shot' humour at the expense of a few 'quacks', whom almost no one took seriously; it is a satire of a prominent political phenomenon – the cynicism with which some chresmologues and demagogues gained influence with credulous citizens by reciting oracles of doubtful authenticity. It is important to remember that in societies that make use of divination, expressions of disbelief are normal; in fact, identifying false sources of prophecy helps sustain belief in true ones. When the Athenians became furious with the chresmologues who had encouraged the Sicilian Expedition, they did not abandon all trust in divination; they were simply angry with the diviners who had failed to use it accurately.[2]

In *Cavalry*, the divination contest has a neatly balanced structure. Paphlagon recites three oracles (1015–20, 1037–40, 1052–3) and is beginning to quote a fourth when he is interrupted by Demos (1059); he alludes to one further oracle (1086–7) and describes a dream he claims to have had (1090–1). For his part, Agorakritos recites four oracles (1030–4, 1055–7, 1067–8, 1080–1), mentions one more (1088–9) and recounts a dream (1092–5).

Paphlagon and Agorakritos each fetch a large number (cf. 999) of oracle texts, probably rolls of papyrus contained in chests (cf. 1000). Paphlagon claims his oracles come from the famous seer Bacis (1003), and Agorakritos ludicrously ascribes his to Glanis ('catfish'), supposedly the elder brother of Bacis (1004). The name Glanis, quite apart from its humorous meaning, rhymes with Bacis, creating the suspicion that Agorakritos' oracles are pure invention. The latter is also suggested by the different textual qualities of the two collections. Paphlagon's oracles combine specific parody of several famous oracular verses with pastiche of epic and epinician poetry. By contrast, Agorakritos' 'oracles', such as they are, do not involve parody of any known oracular texts. The first two respond humorously to Paphlagon's oracles, and the second two, whose interpretations are all but nonsensical, are merely generalized pastiche of oracular language.

The difference between the two collections of oracles is hinted at when Demos asks what the oracles will tell him (1005–10):

Demos   [*To Paphlagon*] But what are they [the oracles] about?

Paphlagon   About Athens, about Pylos, about you, and me, about each and every issue.

Demos   [*To Agorakritos*] And what are yours about?

Agorakritos   About Athens, about lentil soup, about the Lacedaemonians, about fresh mackerel, about men in the agora who cheat when measuring barley meal, about you, and me. He [*pointing to Paphlagon*] can go and suck a dick!

Paphlagon's list of topics is vague and self-aggrandizing but not unsuitable for assembly business. Agorakritos' response jumbles oracles about the war together with everyday concerns about foodstuffs and dishonest market-traders. Although the latter were not without political relevance (Athens' grain supply during the Peloponnesian War was a matter of the highest importance), Agorakritos' words are recipe for popular appeal that demolishes Paphlagon's more serious tone and ends with an obscene insult; as so often, Paphlagon fails to reply in kind and Agorakritos is characterized as cruder than his adversary.

From the very beginning, therefore, the divination contest satirizes the business of chresmologues and the demagogue who cites their oracles, suggesting that their activities are a hoax played on a gullible public. That this is encouraged by the attitudes of the Athenian assembly is strongly implied by Demos' next words (1011–13):

Demos   Come on, both of you read them to me, especially the one I like, about how I'll become 'an eagle amidst the clouds' above!

Demos is mostly concerned to hear one particularly flattering (but apparently genuine) oracle that he has heard before: he is less interested in divine guidance than self-gratification, hardly an auspicious start for a judge of a contest in oracular interpretation. The oracle behind

Demos' words (or at least several verses of it) is quoted by the scholiast (Σ 1013):

Blessed citadel of Athene goddess of the line of battle,
When you have seen much, suffered much, and striven much,
You shall become an eagle amidst the clouds for all time.

The scholiast's note adds that this oracle was mentioned by Aristophanes in *Banqueters* (fr. 241 Henderson) and in *Birds*, where the phrase 'an eagle in the clouds' appears twice (978, 987). Clearly, this oracle was very well known in the late fifth century, and it was probably an oracle of Bacis (cf. *Birds* 960–80). But it is also clear that the famous verses, as they stand, offer nothing more than a vague prognostication of troubles ending in ever-lasting glory – something that no doubt appealed to Athenians in the Peloponnesian War, but can hardly, on its own, have contained much value for political deliberation (though one can imagine that it might have been used to bolster Cleon's obdurate refusal to make peace with Sparta).

Demos' self-deluding desire to hear flattering oracular verses is only the first instance of what is revealed in this episode as a predisposition to misuse and misunderstand divination. He shows himself singularly unskilled in oracular interpretation. Not only does he prejudice the whole practice of divination by declaring what he wants to hear before he has heard it (1011–13; 1065–6, cf. 1078), but he is frequently baffled and helpless (1021, 1041, 1048, 1061, 1072, 1074, 1082), and when he does venture an interpretation or reaction of his own it is usually inspired by a naïvely literal understanding of the enigmatic, metaphorical language of oracles (1022, 1028–9, 1044, 1069). The last is the opposite of how ancient Greeks were accustomed to approach oracular interpretation. In the words of the poet Heraclitus (fr. 93 D-K), 'The god of Delphi [i.e. Apollo] neither tells nor conceals but indicates by signs'. Demos' interpretative efforts fall comically short of the challenge of divining the meaning of oracular verse.

There are three sequences in the divination contest. The first is the longest, and in it Paphlagon has the initiative and recites four oracles:

each oracle is shorter than the last (maintaining the pace of the episode after the initial novelty for the audience has worn off) and every one of them is about himself. The first three encourage Demos to protect him; the last has to do with his victory at Pylos but is interrupted by Demos after only four words. Agorakritos' responses are varied: he reinterprets Paphlagon's first oracle and produces a different one; he offers a different interpretation of Paphlagon's second oracle; he deflates the third with some humorous pseudo-oracular verses; and interprets the fourth one for Demos even before Paphlagon finishes it.

To understand fully the humour and the satirical bite of the divination contest it is crucial to grasp that it is written in two different poetic rhythms (cf. Platter 2007: 114–23). In classical Greece, oracles, whether issued from Apollo's temple at Delphi or elsewhere, were poems, composed in 'dactylic hexameters' (the meter of epic poetry like Hesiod and Homer). The dactylic hexameter sounds very different from the basic meter of 'speech' in drama (the 'iambic trimeter'). Hearing the distinction between the two meters would have been easy for the Athenian audience. Halfway through the first sequence of the divination contest the rhythmic distinction between the poetry of oracles and ordinary speech breaks down, as Agorakritos and Paphlagon begin to 'speak' in dactylic hexameters. The effect of this on stage is to make it appear to the audience that Paphlagon and Agorakritos have begun to adapt epic verse from memory or to invent freely – in other words, they seem to be making up oracles rather than reading them from their collections. This is an indication that not only are oracles of Bacis (let alone Glanis!) bogus and deceptive, but that politicians are fully capable of inventing their own prophetic verses.

Paphlagon's first offering is a six-line hexameter oracle instructing the Athenians to protect 'the sacred, sharp-fanged dog' who provides them with pay (1015–20):

Paphlagon Be mindful, son of Erechtheus, of the track of oracles, which Apollo
Among tripods invaluable cried out to you from his temple.

He enjoined you to protect the sacred, sharp-fanged dog,
Who gapes before you and, shouting out clever things on your behalf,
Provides you with pay. Indeed, if he does not do this, the dog shall die,
For out of hatred many jackdaws caw at him.

The first two lines claim the authority of Apollo and his temple at Delphi. The invocation of Apollo is repeated in several subsequent oracular quotations in this episode (cf. 1024, 1047, 1072, 1081, 1084). It is intended to endow the verses that follow it with the highest divine authority. The first word in Greek (*phrazeu*) is typical of oracular language: it means 'Be mindful!' or 'Beware!' and is very widely found at the beginning of genuine oracular texts. In addition, the use of a mythical patronymic as an ethnic ('son of Erechtheus', meaning 'the Athenians' because Erechtheus was a mythical king of Athens) is characteristic of oracular verse. In short, the opening of Paphlagon's first oracle sounds genuine but quickly descends into parody in the third verse. Paphlagon refers to himself as a 'dog' – a pun in ancient Greek on Cleon's name – using a phrase from Hesiod (*Works and Days* 604) in which the poet advises that the guard-dog of the house must be kept well fed, a fittingly self-serving allusion.[3] The jackdaws are an image of envy, an element of pastiche perhaps drawn from Pindar (*Nemean Odes* 3.82).

Demos' response is bafflement: he has no idea what the oracle means (1021). Paphlagon interprets it for him: 'I am the dog . . . Apollo has told you to protect me, your dog' (1023–4). Agorakritos offers a different interpretation: Paphlagon has falsified parts of the oracle, and he has the real story about the dog (1025–6). Demos wants to hear the oracle (1028) but ludicrously picks up a stone so that the oracle about the dog will not bite him; perhaps he expects a real dog to appear (1029). This is only the first time that he will display a naïvely literal understanding of oracular verses.

Agorakritos' first 'oracle' uses the same opening as Paphlagon's but alters it grammatically so that it tells Demos to *beware* of 'the dog' (i.e. Cleon/Paphlagon), here named Cerberus (cf. *Peace* 313) after the mythical three-headed dog that guards the gates of the Underworld.

The verses Agorakritos chants suggest that 'the dog' steals from the people of Athens by deceiving them with flattery (1031–2; cf. Edwards 2010: 323) and extorts their allies (1034) – charges against Paphlagon frequently levelled elsewhere in the play. Demos is impressed and declares Glanis better than Bacis (1035) – again, this satirizes the assembly's gullibility, since genuine oracles of Bacis were believed to be divinely inspired, while Glanis is Agorakritos' invention.

Paphlagon's second oracle (1036–40) again warns Demos to protect him, and the verses acquire an aura of solemnity by parodying the famous 'wooden wall' oracle (Herodotus 7.141.3) given to the Athenians before the battle of Salamis. Paphlagon also seems to parody an ancient oracle (Herodotus 5.92β.3) about the birth of Cypselus tyrant of Corinth, and perhaps to allude to a prophetic dream (Herodotus 6.131.2) Pericles' mother dreamed shortly before giving birth to the future Athenian leader.

> **Paphlagon** In sacred Athens a woman shall give birth to a lion,
> Which shall do battle with many gnats on the people's behalf,
> As if defending its cubs. Guard that one,
> Building a wooden wall and iron towers.

For the second time, Demos is baffled by the oracle (1041). Paphlagon explains that he is the lion. Ironically, the image of a lion doing battle with gnats alludes to a well-known fable of Aesop (Perry 255) in which a lion tries to fight a gnat but only succeeds in clawing his own face. The implication is that Paphlagon's attempts to 'fight for' the Athenians are nothing but a failure. Agorakritos reinterprets the verses with two well-aimed quips: the oracle means that Paphlagon intends to become a tyrant and so should be clapped in the stocks (1045–9). Demos agrees (1050).[4]

Paphlagon's third oracular offering alludes to Cleon's victory at Pylos (1051–3):

> **Paphlagon** Do not be persuaded, for envious crows are cawing.
> But hold the hawk dear to you and be mindful of him –
> He who brought you the little fish of the Lacedaemonians all
> trussed-up.

The first line (1051) is metrically significant: it is in hexameters, but it is not clear if it is actually part of the oracle or if it is merely Paphlagon's response to Demos before he begins to recite his next oracle (1052). If the latter, then Paphlagon has begun to extemporize hexameter verse. This will become the running (metrical) joke in this episode, that politicians (and by implication chresmologues) are skilful forgers of oracles.

Agorakritos' rebuttal (1054–7) is a scatological oracular parody incorporating a quotation identified by the scholiast (Σ 1056) as coming from the *Little Iliad*, a now lost epic poem.

> **Agorakritos** Yet this only when drunk did Paphlagon hazard.
> 'Ill-counselled son of Cecrops, why think that a mighty deed?
> "Even a woman can bear burden, whenever a man bestows it on her.
> But she can't go into battle": she'd shit herself if she did!'

Line 1055 is a parody of oracular language. 1056 and perhaps the first half of 1057 quote the epic poem mentioned above but descend in 1057 from the epic register into humorous scatological verse.[5] The line that introduces this 'oracle' (1054) is especially significant. Here, Agorakritos clearly satirizes oracles of chresmologues by inventing a hexameter line: it cannot be part of the oracle because it answers Paphlagon's allusion to his victory at Pylos in the previous verse. From this point the audience will begin to hear Agorakritos and Paphlagon undermining the authority of their oracles by revealing that they can converse in spontaneous hexameter verses.

Paphlagon's last effort is to begin another verse about Pylos (1059), but he is cut off by Demos after only four words. Apparently Paphlagon is about to quote the popular saying (Strabo 8.3.7) 'There is a Pylos before Pylos, and there is another Pylos too' (there were three places in the Peloponnese called Pylos). But Demos interrupts, asking, 'What does "before Pylos" mean?', and Agorakritos invents a hexameter punning on the word Pylos (1060): 'He says he's going to take all the pails [(Gk.) *puelous*, which sounds like Pylos] from the bathhouse!' Ironically, Paphlagon's use of this well-known verse is ill-chosen: one implication of it is that there is nothing special about Pylos – there are several of them. Moreover, it piles up a suffocating number of Pylos references, as no doubt Cleon had in political speeches after his victory.

The second sequence of the divination contest is introduced by Agorakritos. He produces an oracle about the fleet, to which he says Demos must pay heed. His words have shifted back into iambic trimeters (1063–4), the ordinary rhythm of speech, showing that he is not inventing oracular verses at this point. Demos prejudices the interpretation of the oracle by telling Agorakritos that above all it must tell him how the sailors will get their pay (1065–6). The old man has already shown himself a clueless interpreter of oracles (cf. 1021–2, 1041), and now he even demands that they mean what he wants before he hears them – an attitude that could only encourage the kind of inventive forgery that Agorakritos and Paphlagon have displayed. Agorakritos recites two hexameters (1067–8):

> **Agorakritos**   Son of Aegeus, beware the dog that is a fox, in case he tricks you,
> The traitorous, swift-footed, cunning, trickster, who is skilled in many ways.

The next line (1069) is important since it is another hexameter, but this time it is divided between Agorakritos and Demos (lines like this are described by the Greek term *antilabē*).

> **Agorakritos**   Do you know what this means?
>
> **Demos**   The fox-dog is Philostratos.

Here, Demos begins to invent hexameters in imitation of Paphlagon and Agorakritos. He enjoys the contest but he still shows no aptitude for deciphering the enigmatic verse of prophecy. His identification of the 'fox-dog' as Philostratos, a well-known pimp who had the nickname Fox-Dog, is another literal (and therefore misguided) interpretation.[6] Agorakritos must explain the 'true' meaning of the 'fox-dog' (1070–6): it is a trireme which, like a dog, moves swiftly, and has rowers who are like foxes, because they eat grapes from vineyards (i.e. while foraging

during expeditions). Agorakritos' explanation is extremely obscure, to
the point of being nonsensical. Demos' response shows how puzzled he
remains (1078): the extra-metrical remark, 'O-*kay* …' (Gk. *eien*),
indicates a pause while his mind turns over Agorakritos' interpretation
of the oracle.[7] He is still preoccupied about how the rowers will receive
their pay – Agorakritos' oracle has not told him what he wanted to
hear.

In the conclusion of this sequence, Agorakritos chants two
hexameters (1080–1) that call themselves an oracle of Apollo; they are
about keeping away from Cyllene, a city in Elis in the Peloponnese. It is
not clear whether these lines are meant to be an oracular text or whether
they are intended as more off-the-cuff invention, but the latter is
suggested by the subsequent exchange in which Demos, Agorakritos
and then Paphlagon discuss the matter in hexameters, each clearly
extemporizing their verses. The 'oracle' contains a pun that is very
difficult to translate: Cyllene sounds like a Greek word meaning
'crooked'. As in the case of the 'fox-dog' oracle, Agorakritos offers a
wildly implausible explanation: Cyllene, he claims, is a metaphor for
Paphlagon's hand, a 'crooked hand' (i.e. cupped) that he holds out like a
beggar expecting money.

Paphlagon's response momentarily seizes the initiative when he tells
Demos that the 'crooked hand' means the hand of Diopeithes, a
contemporary oracle-expert and political figure well known for his
extreme religiosity. He moved a decree to impeach unbelievers and
philosophers who studied the heavens. In *Birds* (988) he is referred to
as 'the great Diopeithes', confirming that he was well-known and
perhaps implying that he had an inflated opinion of himself.[8] It appears
from the lines in *Cavalry* discussed here that either he did indeed have
a crooked (i.e. crippled) hand, or perhaps that he was well-known for
asking (by cupping his hand) for excessive remuneration for his skills in
divination. If the latter is right, then Paphlagon's words imply a privately
sceptical view of oracles and oracular interpretation that reveals
cynicism in his use of divination to persuade Demos.

In the final and shortest phase of the divination contest (1086–99), Paphlagon promises Demos an oracle about how he is to become an eagle and rule the world (1086–7); his words are in hexameters, again showing that the invention of oracular verses is an easy trick. By this point, the metrical distinction between direct speech and oracular quotation has been obliterated. After Agorakritos makes a competing and excessive promise (similarly invented), Paphlagon claims to have had a prophetic dream in which Athene showered the people of Athens with 'health and wealth' (1090–1). Agorakritos answers (1092–5) with another dream that foresaw Demos showered in ambrosia and Paphlagon in 'garlic salt-water' (1095, cf. 199).[9] The dreams are described in hexameters, once more accentuating the point that the verse form of oracles is easily fabricated by unscrupulous demagogues.

Demos is delighted with Agorakritos' dream and shouts with glee in an extra-metrical line, creating an emphatic pause (1096). He declares Glanis the wiser of the two seers. Agorakritos has won another victory: Demos entrusts himself to Agorakritos to 'teach me in old age' and 're-educate me as though I were a boy' (1096–9).[10] This new honour hints, for the first time, at the denouement of the play in which Agorakritos will restore Demos to his former glory. It is also a striking example of the theme of the inversion of social categories, as the old man turns out to need education in the way that only a child usually would.

Paphlagon begs for one more chance to keep his place as Athens' leading demagogue (1100). He asks for a contest in providing Demos with food and a daily living. As so often in the play, political power and success (and corruption) are symbolized by food. Paphlagon promises barley grains but is rejected and offers hulled barley instead (1102–4); Agorakritos trumps his offer with the promise of a meal already prepared (1105–6); and Demos sets the stage for the final contest, which he defines as one in public service (Gk. *eu poiein*: 1108; see Chapter 7). He tells the competitors that whoever wins will take 'the reins of the Pnyx': that is, assume control of the democratic assembly as Athens' top demagogue (1109).

Duet (1111–50)

Together the chorus and Demos sing a lyric ode known by the Greek term as an 'amoebaean'; it is a song in which the singer alternates between two parts and may be termed a 'duet'. The duet separates the oracle contest from the final competition before Agorakritos' victory over Paphlagon. Most surprisingly, Demos informs the chorus that his apparent stupidity and gullibility are part of an act designed to get the most out of politicians before getting rid of them.

The chorus sings first, telling Demos that although he is glorious and feared like a tyrant,[11] he is easily flattered and deceived (1116–17; cf. Edwards 2010: 323), he gapes open-mouthed at speakers, and his mind is, as it were, 'out to lunch' (1111–20). Demos' response (1121–30) is a stinging rebuke to the cavalry, drawing attention to the aristocratic fashion of growing their hair long (cf. 580): they have no brains under their long locks if they cannot see that he only pretends to be deceived by demagogues (cf. 822, 859, 1044, 1102–3). Demos likes flattery and bribery because it gives him pay and he enjoys feeding up thieving politicians so that he can later profit in court by convicting them.

In the second half of the duet, the chorus praises Demos for his cunning ruse of fattening up politicians on the Pnyx like victims for public sacrifice (1131–40) and Demos agrees that his strategy is a clever one. Though he is thought foolish, he only pretends not to see what is going on, before using the courts to make politicians vomit up what they have stolen (1141–50).[12] Demos' description of his manipulation of politicians may echo the 'Old Oligarch' or Pseudo-Xenophon's criticisms of Athenian democracy ([Xenophon], *Constitution of the Athenians* 1.1, 6–9; Brock 1986: 25).

Is Demos a half-suspecting dupe who claims he knows what is going on rather than admit that he is clueless? Or is he fully aware of his surroundings, cynically pretending, all the while, not to notice? If the audience think the latter, can they trust anything that he says in the play from this point forward?[13]

7

Cavalry 1151–1315: Competition in Public Service and Second Parabasis

The final contest between Paphlagon and Agorakritos is a competition in public service, represented by a banquet served for Demos. The result is decided when it comes to light that Paphlagon has stolen from Demos, while Agorakritos, with true public spirit, has given the old man everything he has. Paphlagon makes one final attempt to save himself, testing the sausage-seller against his Delphic oracle to determine whether Agorakritos is the man destined to be his successor. In a sequence steeped in paratragedy, the oracle is found to be fulfilled and Paphlagon's leadership of Athens is over.

With Paphlagon defeated, Agorakritos leads Demos offstage, where the old man will be transformed for the final episode. The audience is given no clue to what is about to happen; instead, there are several indications that Agorakritos will become a demagogue even worse than Paphlagon. In the meantime, the chorus performs the second parabasis (1264–1315), ridiculing several prominent Athenians.

Episode (1151–1263)

This episode falls into two sequences of action. In the first ('the banquet'), Paphlagon and Agorakritos compete as waiters serving Demos, and Paphlagon loses when he is found to have stolen food from his master (1151–1228). In the second ('the elenchus', an examination by question and answer), the Delphic oracle confirms Agorakritos as the man destined to defeat Paphlagon (1229–52), he is crowned as victor (1250–2) and empowered to re-educate Demos and punish

Paphlagon (1259–60). Many important motifs reappear here: politicians act as slaves of the people, Demos thinks of them as his lovers (1162–3), outrageousness is a winning strategy in the competition (1206), food is a metaphor for political success and favour, and the result of the contest is confirmed by an oracle (1229–30).

The banquet sequence is divided into three parts. In the first, Paphlagon and Agorakritos bring out dishes and compete to present them in ingenious and humorous ways (1168–89). In the second, Paphlagon almost wins the competition by serving up a dish of hare's meat, but Agorakritos steals it and serves it to Demos himself (1190–1205). Third and finally, Demos judges the competition by inspecting the contents of the 'picnic-baskets' (literally, 'boxes'; cf. 1211) belonging to the contestants (1207–23).

As a metaphor for public service, the banquet reflects the play's pervasive use of the imagery of food to represent political power, success and corruption (see Chapter 3). To understand the symbolism of a banquet for the people it must be remembered that Athens, at the time *Cavalry* was first performed, did not routinely distribute handouts of food (except at public sacrifices), much less the cash to buy it. A dole of two obols for citizens to spend on subsistence was only instituted later in the war (410 BCE) by the demagogue Cleophon ([Aristotle] *Athenian Constitution* 28.3). Instead of free grain, the city preferred, where possible, to ensure an adequate supply at low prices, and to provide citizens with ways to earn money to spend on it, such as state-pay for trireme rowers, dockyard workers and jurors. References to disappointing promises of grain found in *Cavalry* (1100–3) and *Wasps* (715–18) suggest that Demos' banquet – not just grain or even hulled grain (cf. 1104) given directly to the people, but a fully prepared meal (cf. 1105–6) – is a metaphor for extreme demagogic populism.

Paphlagon defines the banquet contest as a competition in 'euergetism' (Gk. *euergetein*, 1153) or public benefaction. The word is not widely found in Aristophanes (cf. *Wealth* 835, 912, 913) and is part of the technical language of the Athenian democracy. In honorary decree inscriptions it is reserved for cases of exemplary public service to Athens. For example, in an inscription of 409 BCE, the men who assassinated the oligarch Phrynikhos (cf. Thucydides 8.92.2; Lysias 13.70-2) and so helped to rescue Athens' democracy are recorded as 'euergetists' or public benefactors (*IG* i³ 102.20-1, 28 = M-L 85). By contrast with Paphlagon, Agorakritos and Demos talk about the contest with the Greek words *eu poiein* (1108, 1160), a very common phrase with the general sense of 'doing good'. Demos also sees the competition as a continuation of the love contest in the agon. He is determined to be made very happy by his 'lovers' or else: '. . . if not, I'm going to play hard to get!' (1162-3). The rare word (Gk.) *thruptein* contains the idea of coy pretence (e.g. Plato, *Phaedrus* 228c). After the recent revelation that Demos deliberately inveigles politicians into corruption before delighting in their fall (1125-30), the audience might wonder if this is the first evidence that he meant exactly what he said.

In contrast to the second agon, in which every gift but one came from Agorakritos, here the stage action is more balanced and the anxiety over the outcome heightened, as both sides tempt Demos with offerings of food. As the banquet is served, Paphlagon attempts twice to associate his dishes with his victory at Pylos (1167, 1172), and Agorakritos counters with the humorous attribution of dishes to Athene, who is imagined to be cooking Demos' banquet. He offers Demos loaves of bread of gigantic proportions, supposedly baked by the colossal statue of Athene that stood in the Parthenon on the acropolis (1168-9); meat boiled by the goddess (1178); various kinds of tripe that she is said to have cut up (1179, 1184); and wine mixed by Athene herself (1189). Paphlagon tries to trump his adversary with his own invocations of Athene, but Agorakritos' increasing popularity with Demos is indicated by the fact that in this phase of action the old man speaks only to him, never to Paphlagon (cf. 1170, 1175-6, 1181, 1183, 1188).

In his attempts to gain Demos' attention, Paphlagon uses exaggerated epithets of Athene: 'Fighter at Pylos' at 1172, 'Terrifier of Armies' at 1177, and 'Gorgon-Crested one' at 1181. Agorakritos responds with invocations of Athene of his own, 'Daughter of the almighty father' (i.e. daughter of Zeus) at 1178 and 'Tritogenes' at 1189 (i.e. 'born in lake

Tritonis'). While the epithets of Athene that Agorakritos uses are familiar ones, those used by Paphlagon are obscure: they may be intended to sound self-serving (as 'Fighter at Pylos' in 1172 surely is) or even invented (cf. Anderson 1991: 149 n.1). Agorakritos' last epithet of Athene 'Tritogenes' wins the game with one of the goddess's familiar titles turned into a brilliant pun: the wine he serves to Demos, mixed with water following the usual Greek practice, was 'titrated by Tritogenes!' (1189). Paphlagon's one attempt at a pun falls flat (1181–2): Demos is unamused by the suggestion that eating 'ship's biscuit' will lead to smooth sailing for Athens' ships. He appears increasingly marginalized in the contest for Demos' favour.

One exchange between Agorakritos and Demos in this phase of action deserves further comment. As Agorakritos brings Demos a pot of broth, his second mention of Athene ('... manifestly the goddess watches over you: even now, she holds over you a pot of broth', *Cavalry* 1173–4) reminds Demos of some famous lines of the sixth-century Athenian poet and democratic political reformer Solon (fr. 4.3-4 Gerber):

> '... the proud guardian, Pallas Athene, daughter of the almighty father, holds her hands over [the city].'[1]

Our knowledge of these verses comes from the fourth-century orator Demosthenes (19.255), who quotes them at length. Solon's poem is a warning to the Athenians that destruction will come not from the gods but from corrupt leaders of the people. Many of the examples of corruption in it echo allegations made against Paphlagon in *Cavalry*. For instance, Solon says bribery will lead the citizens of Athens to destroy their city (5–6); the unjust intentions of the leaders of the people will cause them to suffer great pains (7–8); in a metaphor familiar from *Cavalry* (food as corruption), the leaders of the people will cause unrest because they do not know how to moderate their feasting (9–10); and they grow rich by unjust deeds, seizing and stealing from everyone, sparing neither sacred nor public property (11–13). Since Solon was regarded as the father of Athenian democracy, the Athenian audience must have been familiar with his poems. The intertextual implication is clear: Paphlagon is the incarnation of civic ruin.

The second phase of the banquet competition begins with the action that will cause Paphlagon's downfall. He offers Demos a slice of a 'flat-cake' (i.e. unleavened bread), and Agorakritos responds by giving Demos a whole one (1190–1). The discovery of the remainder of Paphlagon's flat-cake, kept hidden in his box, will finally prove his corruption. As his last offering, Paphlagon brings a dish of hare's meat (1192), a rare delicacy and one that Agorakritos cannot match. There are erotic undertones here, since a hare was a typical love-gift from an *erastēs* to his *erōmenos* (e.g. *ARV* 471, a red-figure cup by Makron).

This is the moment for Paphlagon to be tricked in a piece of stage-action and dialogue that explicitly evokes the Pylos campaign for the last time in the play. The use of a trick to defeat a powerful adversary is a motif drawn from 'ephebic' myth (Bowie 1993: 55), suitably expressing Agorakritos' simultaneous achievement of victory and manhood (see Chapter 3 and below). Agorakritos pretends to see ambassadors approaching the stage carrying purses of silver coins (1196–7). Paphlagon must put down the hare's meat and head off in the direction Agorakritos is indicating, while Agorakritos seizes the moment to steal the dish and serve it to Demos (1198–9). Paphlagon returns to find that he has been outwitted and robbed (1200–3):

Paphalgon   I'm ruined. You've stolen what belongs to me!

Agorakritos   By Poseidon, that's what you did with the men from Pylos!

Demos   Pray tell me, how did you think of stealing it?

Agorakritos   The idea was Athene's, but I committed the theft.

For the final time in this sequence, Agorakritos invokes Athene to bless his public services and triumphs. The theme of Pylos has come full circle since Demosthenes complained in the prologue that his victory had been snatched unjustly from him (54–7). Paphlagon exclaims in shock (1206) that he is about to be outdone in 'outrageousness' (Gk. *anaideia*), the culmination of an important theme (see Chapter 4).

Agorakritos seizes the moment to ask Demos to judge the result of the contest. The significance of the moment is underlined by a metatheatrical nod to the audience (1210), as Demos asks to be advised how the spectators can see that he will judge wisely. Until now, Demos has been a figure of ridicule, but now the audience must begin to identify with him: his appeal to them is the first step towards winning their sympathies (Slater 2002: 80). Agorakritos tells Demos to inspect each contestant's box (1211–13). Demos first opens Agorakritos' box and finds it empty – it shows concern for the interests of the people (1216). Paphlagon seems to have kept his box at a distance, perhaps not surprisingly in view of its contents, and Demos walks over to it and opens it up (1217). Paphlagon's box is not empty, and Demos exclaims (1218–20):

> **Demos**   Damn! Look how it's stuffed full of good things!
>   What a massive flat-cake he kept for himself!
>   And he cut me off a piece that was *this* teeny-tweeny!

Demos' exclamation (1220) '*this* teeny-tweeny' (Gk. *tunnoutoni*) is highly emphatic, very rare in ancient Greek, and was no doubt colloquial in Athens, since forms of the word are only known from Aristophanes (cf. *Acharnians* 367; *Clouds* 392, 878; *Women at the Thesmophoria* 745; *Frogs* 139). The 'deictic' suffix (Gk. -*i*) indicates, emphatically, something that the speaker can point to (e.g. 'this one *here*'). Deictics are important in the analysis of Greek drama because they are a textual indication of things that the actors (can) point out, often implying visibility to the audience and therefore giving us an idea of what was (happening) on stage. Here, Demos' words suggest that the actor expresses his outrage at Paphlagon's theft with a gesture indicating the small size of the slice of flat-cake he was given. Comic drama surely incorporated far more and larger gestures than can be deduced from the evidence of the texts. However, the indication of a gesture (by contrast with deictics pointing to an actor or prop) is fairly unusual in Aristophanes (cf. 1354, where

Demos hangs his head in shame) and here it emphasizes the moment when Demos sees proof of Paphlagon's corruption.

Agorakritos explains that this is how Paphlagon has been cheating Demos – giving him a small portion of his thefts, while keeping most for himself (1221–3). When Demos realizes that Paphlagon has been cheating him all along, he says reproachfully, in Doric Greek, the dialect spoken in Lacedaemon and elsewhere (1225):

Demos   'But I garlanded you myself and I gave you gifts!'

Though Aristophanes often stages non-Attic speakers who speak in their own dialects (e.g. the Megarian and the Boeotian characters in *Acharnians* and the Spartans in *Lysistrata*), it is unusual, in passages of ordinary speech, for an Attic-speaking character to drop into a different dialect of Greek (cf. *Peace* 47–8). Here, it must have been a surprise for the audience and have marked Demos' words as especially significant. The scholiast's comments on this line identify two reasons for what Aristophanes wrote (Σ 1225).

There is a surface level to the humour: '[Aristophanes] is making a joke about accepting gifts by writing in Doric.' The joke (cf. 996) depends on the assonance in 'and I gifted' (Gk. *kēdōrēsaman*) and in (Gk. *dōristi*) 'in Doric'. Direct translation into English is difficult, but an English parallel would be 'got away *scot*-free', spoken in a Scottish accent. The effect is to emphasize Demos' outraged astonishment at Paphlagon's theft – after he had been rewarded for his success at Pylos.

There is a deeper level of humour too. The scholiast writes: 'Aristophanes is imitating the helots [i.e. slaves of the Lacedaemonians] when they put a garland on Poseidon.' 'The helots' can be understood to mean the play *Helots*, a lost comic drama tentatively ascribed to Aristophanes' rival Eupolis (T1 Storey); if so, *Cavalry* 1225 is a quotation from a play by Eupolis in which some helots, probably the chorus, garlanded a statue of Poseidon. The line is generally agreed to relate to a poetic dispute (Sommerstein 1980; Storey 2003: 278–303) in which Eupolis claimed that he had collaborated with Aristophanes on *Cavalry*, writing not only 1225 but perhaps significant parts of the whole play

(Σ *Cavalry* 1291 has been taken to mean that Eupolis wrote the second half of the second parabasis). The dispute lasted many years: a fragment of Eupolis' play *Dyers* (fr. 89 Storey), probably produced in the mid 410s, reads:

> 'I wrote *Cavalry* together with the bald guy ... and I gave gifts ...'

The 'bald guy' is Aristophanes (cf. *Cavalry* 550; *Peace* 769–74), and the Greek for 'and I gave gifts' is the same Doric word used in *Cavalry* 1225. Eupolis says that he helped Aristophanes to write *Cavalry* and reminds the audience of an unusual Doric verse that he claims he had written, which Aristophanes had then used in *Cavalry*.

Cratinus, too, became involved. In *Wineskin*, produced the year after *Cavalry*, he is said to have mocked Aristophanes for using Eupolis' material (fr. 213 Storey). Some years later, Aristophanes attacked Eupolis in the parabasis of the revised version of *Clouds* (553–4), probably written in the early 410s: 'Eupolis ... dragged [his play] *Maricas* on stage turning our *Cavalry* horribly inside out like the horrible man he is!', alleging that *Maricas* (421 BCE) was a poor imitation of *Cavalry*. Notably, the use of the possessive adjective 'our' in *Clouds* 554 ('our *Cavalry*') might understood as an admission that Eupolis had indeed collaborated with Aristophanes; however, it could equally be a sarcastic reference to Eupolis' claims of authorship.[2]

Professional rivalries between poets of Old Comedy no doubt had a life of their own offstage. The rivalry of Aristophanes and Eupolis was not an isolated case: we know that Hermippus (fr. 64 Storey) accused Phrynichus of using other poets' material. Audiences surely enjoyed this 'theatre gossip'. One thing that all these accusations show is the high value placed on original writing and ingenuity (see Wright 2012: 70–95).

In the final sequence of this episode (1229–63), Paphlagon questions the sausage-seller about his background, testing his answers against the verses of his 'Pythian oracle' (1229), which foretells the identity of the man who will defeat him. Paphlagon proposes to 'cross-examine' (1232) Agorakritos in an 'elenchus' (Socrates used the term for his pedagogical practice of questioning his interlocutors). The sequence begins with Paphlagon refusing to give up his crown of office before the oracle is proven to be fulfilled (1229–30): serving magistrates wore crowns, and if a magistrate was condemned for misconduct, he was immediately stripped of his crown (cf. Demosthenes 26.5; 58.27). The sausage-seller replies that the oracle will be found to declare his name (1231), reminding the audience that they do not yet know what this character is called.

The discovery of the truth of an oracle and its terrible consequences is a type-scene from tragedy. The most famous example is found in Sophocles' *Oedipus Tyrannus* (1121–85), where Oedipus finds he has killed his father and married and had children by his mother. In this passage of *Cavalry*, much of the humour is created by paratragedy. Except when questioning the sausage-seller directly, Paphlagon speaks his lines in tragic rhythm and using tragic vocabulary. His words draw on at least four tragic plays: three of Euripides and one of Sophocles (Aristophanes may have used others that we do not know about). The effect is one of bathetic despair and self-pity, as well as humorous deflation of the dignity of the tragic genre.

In the elenchus (1232–52), Paphlagon at first uses tragic speech without parody of any known lines of tragedy (1232–8); but after the sausage-seller's second answer ('I learned to steal and swear without blinking that I hadn't done it', 1239), he quotes a verse from Euripides' play *Telephus* (fr. 700 Collard-Cropp), 'Oh, Phoebus Apollo, god of Lycia, what yet will you do to me?' (*Cavalry* 1240).[3] As the elenchus reaches its climax and Paphlagon's fate is confirmed, the comic effect of paratragedy intensifies. The sausage-seller's third proof ('Growing up, I sold sausages and now and then myself', 1242) pushes Paphlagon into a longer exclamation of tragic self-pity (1243–4) and elicits his final question: 'Did you sell sausages in the agora or at the city gates?' The answer ('I sold them at the city gates, where salt-fish is sold', 1247) seals Paphlagon's fate and produces his greatest mock-tragic outburst.

First, Paphlagon quotes a line that the scholiast (Σ 1248) ascribes to Sophocles (fr. 885a Lloyd-Jones): 'Alas, the oracle of the god has come to pass!' (1248). Next, he burlesques a verse from Euripides' *Bellerophon* (fr. 311 Collard-Cropp), altering it to include a metatheatrical reference to the (Gk.) *ekkyklēma*, the rolling platform which could be moved in and out of the scene-building: ('Wheel the unlucky one within!', 1249): the humour, here, relies on the fact that tragedy, unlike comedy, avoids breaking the theatrical illusion with direct reference to the mechanics of the stage.[4]

In his final words in the play (1250–2), Paphlagon produces a parody of Euripides' *Alcestis*:

> **Paphlagon**   Oh, garland, farewell! Unwillingly do I leave you.
> Some other man will take and possess you –
> Not more of a thief than I, but perhaps luckier.

Here, the phrase 'Oh, garland, farewell!' is only loosely adapted from *Alcestis* 177–9 ('My marriage bed … farewell!'), but it introduces an unmistakeable parody of *Alcestis* 181–2 ('Some other woman will possess you – not one more virtuous than I, but perhaps luckier'), in which Aristophanes substitutes only two words from Euripides' verse and alters the grammatical gender of a third. Satirical bite is added by the fact that the word 'virtuous' (Gk. *sōphrōn*) in *Alcestis* 182 is exchanged for 'thief' in *Cavalry* (1252), emphasizing Paphlagon's lack of *sōphrosynē* (see Chapter 4).

Paphlagon presumably drops his garland at 1250, ready for the sausage-seller to pick it up and crown himself at 1253, a symbol of victory and celebration. The *ekkyklēma* has probably been rolled (cf. 1249) into the *skēnē* by this point (1252), if *Cavalry* observes the three-actor convention (see Chapter 3), because the actor playing Paphlagon must reappear briefly as Demosthenes, perhaps popping his head out of the *skēnē* after a change of mask (1254–6). He asks Agorakritos to remember that he has made him a man (cf. 177–9; see Chapter 3), completing the sausage-seller's transformation from nobody to the leader of Athens; this is confirmed later when Demos calls Agorakritos 'dearest among men' (1335). By contrast, Paphlagon's last words, casting him as Alcestis in Euripides' drama, have implicitly feminized him, as though in defeat he is no longer a man at all.

Demosthenes' last words (1255–6) suggest that, like Paphlagon, he is anticipating the sausage-seller's leadership to be just as corrupt as his predecessor's, if not more so, since he asks to become a Phanos to Agorakritos, meaning that he hopes to be a 'signatory of accusations' on behalf of the new demagogue-in-chief. Phanos was an historical individual; he is mentioned in *Wasps* (1220) as an associate of Cleon, but whether he did indeed bring lawsuits on behalf of Cleon is not known. Once more, Demosthenes' request misleads the audience about the play's denouement: the oracle in the prologue predicted an ever-worsening succession of demagogues, but nothing yet anticipates what sort of leader of Athens the sausage-seller will turn out to be.

In the final lines of the episode, Demos asks the sausage-seller his name, and at last this character is revealed as Agorakritos (1257). The name is known in ancient Greek but is rare: it is not attested as the name of any Athenian in the classical period (cf. *LGPN* p. 8.). One possible meaning of 'Agorakritos' is 'Chosen by the Assembly', fittingly for the sausage-seller's new relationship to Demos. But Agorakritos etymologizes his name differently, explaining that he was so called because he was 'nurtured with arguments in the agora' (1258). Again, the intention is to make the audience think that Agorakritos truly is a demagogue worse than Paphlagon, heightening the surprise effect of the final episode.

Demos entrusts himself to Agorakritos and turns Paphlagon over to him for punishment (1259–60). Agorakritos' response is ambivalent. He promises Demos, 'I will take good care of you' (1261), adding that Demos will agree that he has never seen 'a better man for the city' (1262–3). Even to the casual listener in the audience, Agorakritos' words must have been troubling, for when he mentions the city, he does not call it the city 'of the Athenians' but 'of the Mouthenians', punning on the Greek word for 'gape open-mouthed' (Gk. *khaskein*), a common image of gullibility (see Chapter 5).[5] To the attentive reader, Agorakritos' promise is yet more concerning, for the word for 'taking care' (Gk. *therapeuein*) is otherwise only found twice in the play. In both cases it characterizes the relationship Paphlagon cultivates between himself and Demos (59, 799). Therefore, the episode ends on a disturbing note: Agorakritos' words suggest that he is going to take over precisely where Paphlagon left off as an even more corrupt Athenian demagogue, just as the oracle in the prologue predicted.

Second parabasis (1264–1315)

The second parabasis occupies the time on stage while, unbeknownst to the audience, Agorakritos is saving the city by transforming Demos. When Aristophanes writes a second parabasis, it is shorter and simpler than the first, lacking the long anapaestic speech that introduces and defines the main parabasis. This means that the second parabasis is structured as an epirrhematic syzygy, like an agon or the second part of the main parabasis (see Chapter 4).

The second parabasis begins with the first of a pair of strophic odes; each is written in a complex lyric metre called 'dactylo-epitrite'. It was favoured by the epinician (i.e. 'victory') poet Pindar, and so it is appropriate that the first ode begins with an adaptation of some verses of Pindar (fr. 89a Snell-Maehler): 'What lovelier way is there to begin or end our song than with deep-girdled Leto and [Artemis] the driver of swift horses?' Pindar's lyrics are adapted to mock two men: 'What lovelier way to begin or end our song, as drivers of swift horses, than to sing nothing about Lysistratos or Thoumantis?' (1264–8). The point is that epinician poetry like Pindar's is for men who deserve praise and glory – unlike Lysistratos and Thoumantis.

Thoumantis is mocked for being desperately hungry and poor (1270–3), so much so that he goes to Delphi to claim sanctuary by supplication at Apollo's statue; similarly, Hermippus (fr. 36 Storey) describes Thoumantis as extremely thin. Claiming sanctuary is the first of a series of 'supplication' images that runs through the second parabasis. Supplication is a ritual act of claiming protection (see Gould 1973). It appears in two forms: one for supplication of a god, another for supplicating a human. In each form, physical contact is essential. Supplicating a god requires contact with somewhere sacred to that god, like an altar or statue. Supplication of a person requires clasping their knees. In each form, the suppliant is placed under divine protection – anyone who broke the physical contact that enabled supplication or refused the suppliant's plea had the wrath of Zeus Hikesios, the god of suppliants, to fear.

Lysistratos is a very common name, so it is uncertain who is singled out here; but it is likely that he is the same man mocked by Aristophanes in *Acharnians* (854–9) and *Wasps* (787–95, 1308–13). In these passages, Lysistratos is ridiculed for his poverty, for cheating others out of small amounts of money, and for going around poorly dressed. *Wasps* 1308–13, where Lysistratos appears in the narrative of a symposium making jokes about other guests, suggests that he might have been a 'parasite', living off the generosity of a wealthy man. These 'professional dinner guests' were expected to be entertaining at parties and to support their patrons in public. If a parasite was attached to a famous patron, he could quickly have become well known.

It is not impossible that Lysistratos and Thoumantis were genuinely poor and notorious for the remarkably ragged and emaciated state in which they went about in public. In Thucydides (2.40.1), Pericles says that in Athens poverty is only shameful if a man does nothing about it. Yet poverty must have affected very large numbers of Athenians, so it is unclear why Aristophanes singles out these two men. One possibility is that they were in fact rich – misers who tried to avoid liturgies or other public contributions of money by pretending to be poor (cf. *Frogs* 1065–6). If so, they are targeted here for failing to fulfil their proper civic role, an accusation that would continue the theme of public service from the previous episode.

The interpretation of the first speech (1274–89) is vexed. The chorus-leader claims to be a friend of the well-known lyre-player Arignotos, but then turns, in an unfriendly way, to accusing Arignotos' brother Ariphrades of enjoying 'eating out' prostitutes in brothels. He concludes that he will never share a drinking-cup with anyone who is not utterly disgusted with Ariphrades.

The name Ariphrades is very rare (cf. *LGPN* p. 63) and his identity as son of Automenes and brother of Arignotos is not in doubt. More information about Ariphrades' family is found in the second parabasis of *Wasps* (1275–83), where it is explained that Automenes had three 'exceptionally talented' sons: Arignotos the lyre-player, a brother (name unknown) who was an actor, and Ariphrades who 'taught himself, his father once swore, to use his tongue every time he went into a whorehouse' (*Wasps* 1281–3). It seems, then, that Automenes and sons were a family heavily involved in music and theatre in Athens, much like the family of the tragic poet Carcinus, whose sons, all talented dancers, are ridiculed at the end of *Wasps* (1498–1532).[6] The family of Automenes would then differ from that of Carcinus mainly because one son was talentless and unremarkable, apart from his sexual predilections. But there is a possibility that Ariphrades was a comic dramatist, and therefore a rival of Aristophanes (Ariphrades T1 Storey).

In the *Poetics*, Aristotle mentions a comic poet called Ariphrades, and since the name is so rare, it is not unlikely that this is the same man that Aristophanes is ridiculing. If this is correct, then there might be a poetic explanation for Aristophanes' repeated attacks on Ariphrades (*Wasps* 1280–3; *Peace* 883–5; and, conjecturally, fr. 926 Henderson). Over several years at least, in *Cavalry*, *Wasps* and *Peace* (i.e. 424–21 BCE), Aristophanes returns to the joke that Ariphrades performs cunnilingus on prostitutes. There are few references to cunnilingus in Aristophanes (cf. *Assembly Women* 846–7), and it is possible that a public allegation that a well-known citizen not only enjoyed it but did so in brothels was sufficiently original and heinous to scandalize the Athenian audience and remain memorably funny. However, Aristophanes' description of Ariphrades' activities does not stop at cunnilingus or brothels (1280–7):

> **Chorus-Leader** Now, Arignotos has a brother, but one unrelated to
> him as far as his behaviour goes, Ariphrades the scumbag. But a
> scumbag is what he would *like* to be. In fact, he's not just a scumbag,
> or I would never have noticed him, and he isn't even just a total piece
> of shit … he's invented something beyond that! He revels in

shamelessly covering his tongue in filth, licking the unspeakable 'morning dew' in whorehouses, and getting his beard dirty, and stirring up the 'sacred hearths', and making like Polymnestos, and hanging around with Oionikhos.

The 'morning dew' means vaginal secretion (Henderson 1991: 145), and 'sacred hearth' is a metaphor for the vulva (cf. *Women at the Thesmophoria* 912; Austin and Olson 2004: 291). Less easy to explain are the references to Polymnestos and Oionikhos. The easiest explanation is that they were, like Ariphrades, frequenters of brothels in Athens, with their own sexual predilections the subject of scandalous gossip; but the evidence about them points in a different direction.

Unquestionably, associating Ariphrades with Polymnestos and Oionikhos is meant to be insulting, but why remains unclear. Oionikhos is an obscure figure; he is not mentioned anywhere else in Aristophanes' surviving plays. The phrase 'hanging around with Oionikhos' (1287) makes sense most naturally if Oionikhos was a contemporary figure. His name is very rare (cf. *LGPN* p. 349), so the only other evidence for an Athenian of that name, found in a fragment of an unknown comic poet (Adespota fr. 396 Storey), might relate to the same person: the fragment tells us that Oionikhos had a (Gk.) *mouseion*, perhaps meaning a 'school of music'.

Polymnestos is a very common name; numerous examples of it are known from classical Athens (cf. *LGPN* p. 374). But the scholia on *Cavalry* 1287 do not point to a contemporary Athenian; instead, they make the identification of Polymnestos of Colophon, a famous and long-deceased musician. Little is known about Polymnestos of Colophon, except from a treatise called *On Music* by Pseudo-Plutarch (cf. Totaro 1999: 45–6); he was known for composing poetry to a well-known melody called 'the Orthian' ([Plutarch] *On Music* 1134c). This strengthens the identification of the man referred to in *Cavalry* 1287 as the famous musician because just a few lines earlier (1279) Aristophanes jokes about the Orthian melody. One further reference to Polymnestos survives in the remains of Old Comedy: Cratinus (fr. 338 Storey) says, of some unknown person, that he or she '. . . sings the songs of Polymnestos and is learning music'.

Drawing the evidence together, a picture comes into focus of Ariphrades as an unsophisticated poet. Literally translated, Aristophanes' words in 1287 (Gk. *polymnēsteia poiōn*) do not mean 'making like Polymnestos' but 'making Polymnesteians' (i.e. 'composing in the style of Polymnestos'; cf. [Plutarch], *On Music* 1133a). The fragment of Cratinus quoted above ('. . . singing the songs of Polymnestos and . . . learning music') implies that the songs of Polymnestos were rudimentary works suitable for beginners. Further support is found in Aristotle's description of Ariphrades' comedy (*Poetics* 1485b31-59a3), where Ariphrades is only mentioned because he is an example of a comic writer who made fun of tragic diction in an unsophisticated way. It is difficult to know what to make of the reference to Oionikhos, but if his presumed 'school of music' was thought to be old-fashioned or inferior, the reference to Ariphrades 'hanging around' with him would add to the picture of a dramatist lacking the aptitude for sophisticated poetry.

Is there also a meta-poetic explanation of Ariphrades' activities in brothels? It is not improbable for the syntax of *Cavalry* 1284–7 links 'composing Polymnesteians' and 'hanging around with Oionikhos' directly to them. The statement (1283) that Ariphrades has 'invented something' could be a metaphor for original poetic composition. Similarly, in *Wasps* 1283, Ariphrades is said to have taught himself to 'do things with his tongue' (Gk. *glōttopoiein*) by going into brothels. The Greek word for 'do things with the tongue' also means 'talk' or 'sing' and can even be interpreted as 'compose poetry'. The image of Ariphrades 'singing in brothels' could, then, suggest that he wrote poetry with sexual themes. Moreover, it is possible that *glōttopoiein* contains a pun on *gelōtopoiein*, which means 'raise a laugh', and so by implication could mean not just 'write poetry' but 'write *comedy*' (Sommerstein 1983: 233).

Reading the second parabases of *Cavalry* and *Wasps* together suggests Aristophanes' jibes at Ariphrades have metapoetic implication – perhaps Ariphrades had composed a comic drama about brothels and prostitutes. It remains no more than speculation, but the joke behind Aristophanes' attacks on Ariphrades might have been that he was a poet of little talent, famous only for having a filthy mouth. If, for example, Ariphrades had staged prostitute characters, set a play in a brothel, or written songs for a chorus of prostitutes, the widespread assumption in the ancient world that authors write about what they do in real life will have made it easy for the audience to imagine that Ariphrades' poetic art reflected his life and character.[7]

The final two lines of the speech (1288–9) are attributed by the scholia (Σ 1291) to Eupolis (see above). Possibly the issue is, in fact, parody of Eupolis, if he had a fondness for writing clauses beginning 'Whoever . . .', since the recurrence of these in this speech looks pointed (1275, 1278, 1279, 1288), and another example of this phrasing (*Clouds* 560) directly mocks Eupolis. Mimicry of his poetry might have motivated Eupolis' claim that Aristophanes had needed his help to write *Cavalry* (Hubbard 1991: 85–6).

The antistrophe (1290–9) mocks one of Aristophanes' favourite targets, Cleonymus (see Chapter 5). Here, Cleonymus' gluttony is alleged to have ruined rich men, apparently as an over-demanding dinner-guest, but this is probably a metaphor for tax-collecting or bringing prosecutions against wealthy men. The language of this passage draws on epic poetry, poking fun at Cleonymus for having a heroic-sized appetite. An opposition is drawn with the strophe, where Thoumantis was mocked for his poverty and continual hunger; and strophe and antistrophe reflect each other by thematizing supplication: Thoumantis clutching Apollo's statue at Delphi, the rich men hugging Cleonymus' knees, begging for mercy.

The final speech, like that of the main parabasis, is whimsical in character. In it, Athens' triremes are imagined coming to life and talking among themselves about the demagogue Hyperbolus, who is said to be planning to send one hundred of them to conquer the north-African city of Carthage – a megalomaniac ambition beyond anything that the Athenian Empire ever actually attempted.

The triremes are characterized as unmarried girls (cf. 1302) and much of the humour is generated by their unwillingness to lose their virginity (1307–10):

Chorus-Leader   And [it is said] one of them,
Who had yet to make her maiden voyage, spoke up:
'By Apollo, averter of evil! Never shall Hyperbolus board me and take
    my helm!
If I have to, I'll let myself grow old here, rotten and full of woodworms.'
[And another said,]
'Nor, by all the gods, shall he sail in Nauphante, daughter of Nauson,
Not if my hull too is joined from planks and pine resin!'

They decide, fantastically, to sail over land to the foot of the acropolis
and claim sanctuary by supplication at Temple of Theseus or the shrine
of the Erinyes; the latter were goddesses of vengeance, euphemistically
known as the 'Dread Goddesses'. The ships' refusal to go to war reverses
the horses' willingness to row triremes in the antode of the first parabasis
(Hubbard 1991: 86) and concludes the theme of supplication.

Like Cleon, the demagogue Hyperbolus was in favour of radical
democracy, against making peace with Sparta, and drew his support
from the masses. He was evidently precocious in his political career
(cf. Cratinus fr. 283 Storey; Eupolis fr. 252 Storey), which he probably
began by bringing prosecutions in the courts (cf. *Acharnians*
846–7; *Wasps* 1007). After Cleon's death, Hyperbolus became Athens'
leading demagogue. He was a natural target for comic poets: the comic
dramatists Plato, Eupolis and Hermippus wrote comedy about him (see
Chapter 2). Just as Cleon's wealth was said to have been gained from his
tannery, Hyperbolus was ridiculed for becoming rich from the profits
of a lamp-making business (cf. Cratinus fr. 209 Storey). This motivates
the joke made by the trireme Nauphante at the end of this speech
(1314–15): 'Let Hyperbolus sail off to hell, if that's what he wants, going
to sea in the boxes from which he used to sell his lamps!'

In what is otherwise an entirely male-focused play – *Cavalry* is
unique among Aristophanes' surviving plays in having no speaking
female characters – the chorus' fantasy of the triremes meeting to
discuss and reject Hyperbolus opens a space for female voices to join
with the other opposers of demagoguery (Anderson 2003).

8

Cavalry 1316–1408: Closing Episodes and Exodos

The final sequence of action in *Cavalry* contains two short episodes. The first is a dialogue between Agorakritos and the chorus before Demos returns to the stage transformed. Agorakritos announces that he has cooked Demos, boiling him down to restore the old man to the way he was in the days of the Persian Wars. In the second episode, Agorakritos reminds Demos of his former mistakes, Demos repents and is rewarded, and Agorakritos accepts an invitation to dine in the Prytaneion. There is no choral exodos in *Cavalry*, an unusual feature of the play.

Episode (1316–34)

Immediately before the second parabasis, Agorakritos has led Demos offstage, promising to care for the old man and to be the best friend the city has ever known; but his words (1261–3) have sinister undertones (see Chapter 7). There, and elsewhere, Aristophanes has misdirected the audience about the end of play, repeatedly suggesting that Agorakritos will become a demagogue even worse than Paphlagon, as the oracle in the prologue predicted (128–43; cf. 683–7, 1252, 1255–6). With the second parabasis over, Agorakritos reappears and proclaims a moment of holy joy and celebration. In this episode, he and the chorus chant their lines in an elevated meter (anapaestic tetrameters, rather than the spoken iambic trimeter), in a manner appropriate to the momentousness of the occasion.

Agorakritos' first words 'Keep holy silence and close your mouths' (1316), proclaim the beginning of a religious rite. The words 'close your mouths' answer his earlier characterization of Athens as the city of gaping mouths (1263) –with their mouths closed, the Athenians are about to rid themselves of their gullibility, and Agorakritos will prove their saviour after all, not another in a long line of corrupt demagogues. He also calls for the lawcourts to close (1316–17), which was customary on days of festive rejoicing ([Xenophon], *Constitution of the Athenians* 3.8) and is fitting for the triumph over Paphlagon, for whom jurors were a mainstay of support (cf. 255–7).

Agorakritos appeals to the audience to raise the 'paean' (1318), a traditional song very often sung as a spontaneous expression of triumph (cf. Thucydides 2.91.2). If the audience, perhaps encouraged by the chorus, responded here with the appropriate ritual cry, (Gk.) '*iē paiōn*', it will have been a ringing endorsement of Aristophanes' play just as much as of Agorakritos' victory over Paphlagon.

The chorus address Agorakritos as 'protector of the islands' (1319) – a sharp contrast with Paphlagon, who harms the allied cities of the empire by extorting their representatives (cf. 326, 1034, 1198, 1408). They anticipate that his good news will bring civic sacrifices (1320). Such rites were held only on exceptional occasions, usually in celebration of military victory. Earlier in the play, city sacrifices were proposed, ludicrously, in gratitude for the favourable price of fish in the market (654–62). By contrast, the authentic solemnity here is emphasized by the religious tone of the words 'make smoke in the streets' (1320; cf. *Birds* 1233; Demosthenes 21.51).

In reply, Agorakritos explains that he has 'boiled down' Demos, making him 'handsome instead of ugly' (1321). The idea of cooking an old man is no doubt inspired by two myths about the sorceress Medea. In a lost Homeric poem, Medea rejuvenated her lover Jason's father Aeson by 'boiling many drugs in golden cauldrons' (*Returns* fr. 6.3 West). In a closely parallel tale, Medea tricked the daughters of Pelias into killing their father: Medea cut up and boiled a ram, making it young again; the daughters of Pelias tried to do the same with their father and murdered him (Diodorus 4.52.1-2; Pausanias 8.11.2-3). The association of Agorakritos with Medea may have reignited the audience's anxieties about the kind of leader he will be.

The chorus asks where Demos is and are told that he has gone back to the past, dwelling in the 'violet-crowned' Athens of old (1323). The epithet 'violet-crowned' is drawn from a verse of Pindar (fr. 76 Race); the allusion to the famous poet of epinician is fitting for the glorious success that Agorakritos is relating. The chorus's questions, 'What does he look like? How is he dressed? Who has he become?' (1324), cue the audience to anticipate an eye-catching change of Demos' costume and mask.

The 'Athens of old' is the city of Aristides and Miltiades (cf. 1325), who were famous Athenian leaders of the late sixth and early fifth centuries; their names evoke the era of the Persian Wars (i.e. 490–479 BCE), when Athens played a central role in the defence of Greece. Miltiades, the victor of the battle of Marathon, died a little after 489 BCE and Aristides, the architect of the Delian League, at some point in the years 468–467 BCE; this places the 'Athens of old' more than forty years before the original production of *Cavalry*, an era that only the oldest in the audience would remember with any clarity, but one with which all will have been familiar as an age of ancestral glory. Miltiades and Aristides were aristocratic conservatives ([Aristotle] *Constitution of the Athenians* 28.3), the antithesis of demagogues like Cleon.[1]

The audience is told to 'shout out for joy' (1327) as the Propylaea (the gate of the acropolis) opens. The staging must at least have invited the audience to imagine the *skēnē* to represent the Propylaea (instead of Demos' house), if nothing more sophisticated was engineered, so that Demos descends from the acropolis, the most sacred site in the city. Demos wears an old-fashioned (cf. *Clouds* 984) golden grasshopper brooch in his hair and is costumed 'in the old style' (1331). This probably means that he is now dressed in a long linen tunic (contrasting with the later fifth-century Athenian preference for shorter tunics) and a long cloak (cf. Stone 1981: 403). The earlier fifth-century fashions worn by older men are described by Thucydides (1.6.3). The grasshopper brooch was used to tie the hair up into a knot: therefore, Demos now has long hair like the chorus, a marker of aristocratic identity that was previously an issue of antagonism between them (cf. 1121–3). The grasshopper brooch was a symbol of autochthony, since grasshopper-larvae emerge from the earth; this might suggest that Demos has been purified of foreign elements like Paphlagon.

Demos' appearance, now that he has become 'handsome instead of ugly' (1321) and restored to his former glory, must have been a striking combination of old-fashioned costume with a new mask. There is disagreement over whether he has become young again or simply 'beautified'. Perhaps he wears the mask of a handsome older man, since the grasshopper brooch was a fashion of older men and nothing in the text shows definitively that his face is young.[2] He is also described as redolent of myrrh (i.e. perfumed for a celebratory feast) and libations, (Gk.) *spondai,* a pun since the word means both 'wine offered to the gods' and 'peace treaties', anticipating the cessation of hostilities (something to which Cleon was opposed). The delightful scents contrast with Demos' former odour of mussel shells, which were used in the now-closed courts as voting tokens by Cleon's client-jurors (1332: cf. *Wasps* 349).

Like most of Aristophanes' comedies, *Cavalry* can be seen to end with troubling, ironic notes amid the atmosphere of joy, triumph and celebration. In addition to Agorakritos' magic powers and their association with Medea, Demos, in his new costume, might be thought to have become an aristocrat, indeed one of the most anti-democratic-type: luxurious, non-Greek, even monarchical (cf. 1330, 1337; Wohl 2002: 113–15). There may be irony, too, in the invocation of Athens as 'violet-crowned' and 'gleaming' (1329), since in *Acharnians* Aristophanes criticizes these adjectives as typical of political flattery (*Acharnians* 636–40; Edwards 2010: 328–30; Olson 2002: 238).

Episode (1335–1408)

Cavalry's final episode returns to the ordinary rhythms of speech for a dialogue between Agorakritos and the transformed Demos. Their conversation divides into three sequences. In the first, Agorakritos reminds Demos of his former mistakes (1335–55). In the second, Agorakritos questions Demos about how he intends to behave in future

(1356–83). And in the third, Demos is rewarded, Paphlagon's punishment is decided, and Agorakritos is invited to dine in the Prytaneion (1384–1408).

The episode begins with Demos calling Agorakritos his 'greatest friend' (1335). He asks Agorakritos to come over to him, exclaiming 'What a good thing you did by boiling me down!' (1335–6). Perhaps Agorakritos remains where he is, for Demos has yet to redeem himself by acknowledging his former errors and at this point he appears to have amnesia (1337–9). In what follows, Demos learns how he used to behave when he was an old man and each time responds with a question, suggesting his surprise at his former behaviour (1344, 1346, 1349); the extra-metrical 'What are you saying?' after 1345 creates a break in the flow of the dialogue, emphasizing Demos' shock and embarrassment. But how far he can be trusted after his cynical revelations in the 'duet' (1125–30, 1141–50) and other hints that he is more aware of the machinations of his politician-slaves than he pretends?

Agorakritos' discussion of what Demos used to do focuses on his behaviour in the assembly (cf. 1340). First, he mentions the erotic rhetoric (1340–9) that appealed to Demos earlier in the play and how easily it used to deceive him (see Chapter 5). Agorakritos' example of the erotic language Demos used to enjoy (1341–2: 'Demos, I am your lover and I love you and cherish you') echoes Paphlagon's first use of erotic language in the second agon (732), associating erotic rhetoric with his corrupting influence. The word (Gk.) *kēdomai* ('I cherish') in 1342 is rare in Aristophanes; it strikes a note of bathetic emotional appeal (cf. *Acharnians* 332, 1028; *Clouds* 106, 1410). Notably, Agorakritos makes jokes at Demos' expense (1343–4, 1347–8), something that no character has done before – at least not within earshot of the old man. This suggests that a good leader is not afraid to criticize the assembly and does not constantly pander to its desires.

Next, Agorakritos reminds Demos of how he used to vote when deciding between competing proposals: in this case, whether to vote to spend money on building triremes or on doles of state pay (1350–3). Encouraged by Paphlagon, who used state-pay as an instrument of popular power (cf. 799–800), Demos used to place his short-term self-interest over the long-term interests of the city. The first sequence reaches its close with Demos hanging his head (1354) and admitting that he is ashamed of his mistakes (1355).

In the next sequence (1356–83), Agorakritos inquires how Demos will behave in future, asking two questions. First, what will he do with corrupt prosecutors in lawcourts who threaten juries that they will go unpaid if they fail to convict (1358–61)? This was a well-known defence strategy in Athenian law-court rhetoric (cf. Lysias 27.1): since jury-pay was funded by fines and confiscations of property, juries had an interest in convicting rich men. Clearly, such a practice undermined the theoretical impartiality of juries: the 'dicastic' oath, sworn by jurors, required them, among other things, to refuse bribes, be impartial, and judge the defendant only on the charge against him (cf. Demosthenes 24.149-51). Demos answers the question with a joke about the demagogue Hyperbolus, who has just been ridiculed in the second parabasis (1362–3: 'I'll throw [a prosecutor like that] into the "barathron", with Hyperbolus hung around his neck!'). The barathron was a pit outside the city walls into which men condemned as 'enemies of the people', such as traitors, were thrown (cf. Xenophon, *Hellenica* 1.7.20). The harshness of the punishment reflects the passion with which Aristophanes characteristically satirizes the twin scourges of demagogues and a corrupt court system, here in *Cavalry* and in other plays, notably *Wasps*.

Finally, Agorakritos asks what Demos' policies will be for everything else (1365). In response to this open-ended question, another aspect of Demos' transformation becomes apparent: no longer under the influence of Paphlagon, he begins to think for himself, and Agorakritos' task of being Demos' 'teacher of old age' and re-educating him (1098–9) comes to fruition. Demos becomes the dominant speaker in the dialogue: he lists various practices that will now cease, and Agorakritos reacts with humorous encouragement. His remarks focus on all levels of Athenian society, beginning with the thetes, who will be paid immediately and in full on return from active service, progressing to hoplites, and finally to the aristocratic elite (1366–83). In regard to the hoplites Demos resolves to clamp down on cowardice and favouritism, making a joke about Cleonymus (1369–72):

Demos   …no hoplite whose name is on one list
will be allowed to transfer to another by special pleading.
He will stay where he was originally listed.

Agorakritos   That bit Cleonymus in the shield-strap!

The names of Athenian citizens assigned to military duties were selected from muster lists of men eligible for military service and the names of those called up for duty were displayed on noticeboards in the agora. The complaint here is that a hoplite (armoured infantry) might influence the generals into changing his assignment, no doubt to less dangerous duties. There is little doubt that such things happened. The experiences of a soldier who claimed he was wrongly included in a military list by a general (Lysias 9) illustrate the potential for corruption that the system harboured.

Demos' jibe at Cleonymus suggests he is the kind of man who would try to make a general move his name from one list to another. Cleonymus was one of Aristophanes' favourite targets (see Chapter 7). In addition to other jokes, he is repeatedly ridiculed, for at least a decade from *Cavalry* on, for having thrown away his shield in battle (cf. *Clouds* 353–4; *Wasps* 15–27, 592, 882–3; *Peace* 444–6, 673–8, 1295–1304; *Birds* 289–90, 1473–81). This was an act of cowardice, since throwing away a shield allowed a foot-soldier to escape more easily, and a serious offence: if prosecuted and proven, the penalty was loss of citizenship (cf. Andocides 1.74). So sensitive was the issue, that it was also an actionable slander to say in public that a man had thrown away his shield (cf. Lysias 10.9). It is tempting to speculate that the joke here is that Cleonymus had claimed to have lost his shield because its shield-strap broke.

Demos' account of how he will change his behaviour ends with his decision to forbid youths whose beards have not grown from hanging around in the marketplace (1373). He focuses his criticism on youngsters who loiter near the perfume stalls and discuss rhetoric

(1375–80). The perfume market, like barbers' shops, was well-known for attracting idlers and loiterers (cf. Lysias 24.20; Pherecrates fr. 70 Storey). Demos declares that these young men will be sent hunting, a typically aristocratic pursuit, to stop them from proposing business in the assembly (1382–3). His words here suggest that at last there will be a cessation of the irresponsible assembly rhetoric that has damaged the city under Paphlagon's leadership.

In the final sequence of the episode, Agorakritos rewards Demos for his reformed attitudes with two gifts: first, a well-endowed slave boy who will follow him around carrying a folding chair for him to sit on (1384–6). This prompts Agorakritos to joke that Demos can use the boy like a folding chair if he feels like it – meaning that he can bend him over for anal sex. Demos' response, 'Aren't I fortunate to be going back to the old ways?' (1387), confirms that he is no longer an *erōmenos*, the passive partner of an *erastēs*, as he was in the second agon (Chapter 5), but himself an *erastēs*. The erotic rhetoric that once defined him as an *erōmenos* (cf. 732–3) and deceived him so easily has lost its potency. Secondly, Demos is given peace treaties for thirty years, a long-term solution to the Peloponnesian War (1388–9); they are represented as girls, whom Paphlagon has been hiding in the house out of sight, just as he has long been cheating Demos in other ways. Demos will be able to use them for his sexual gratification (1391), another sign of his return from senescent passivity to more potent virility. This completes the evolution of a sexual theme in *Cavalry*, which began in the prologue with Nicias' reference to Phaedra and Demosthenes pretending to masturbate (see Chapter 3): depreciated forms of sexuality are replaced with triumphantly active homosexual and heterosexual sex.

At last, then, Demos can return to the countryside (1394–5), an image of peace, prosperity and normality (cf. *Peace* 1318; fr. 109 Henderson) after the confinement in the city caused by the Peloponnesian War (cf. *Acharnians* 32). He asks how Paphlagon will be punished. Agorakritos replies that Paphlagon will enter the business of sausage-selling at the city gates, where he himself once plied his trade (1397–1401). Symbolically, the demagogue is removed from the centre of civic life to the margins of the city. The phrase 'at the city gates' (1398) echoes Paphlagon's much-vaunted victory at Pylos, since (Gk.) *pylos* is the word for 'gate', so the place of Paphlagon's exile is ironic as well as fitting. The image of Paphlagon exchanging insults with prostitutes (1400) may point to the location of Paphlagon's new place of work as the 'Sacred Gate' to the northwest of the agora, for the area was known to be frequented by prostitutes (Lind 1990: 175–84; for a map, see Figure 1).

Further irony is found in Demos' insult that Paphlagon is a (Gk.) *pharmakos* (1405) – a 'scapegoat' to be ritually expelled from the city. The Athenians expelled two scapegoats annually at the spring festival called the Thargelia.[3] It is possible, but not certain, that the scapegoats at Athens were lavishly fed at public expense before they were driven out of the city. If the latter is right, then the insult is well-chosen: Paphlagon's expulsion follows the end of the controversial public dining rights that he obtained after the victory at Pylos.[4]

In the final lines of the play, Demos invites Agorakritos (1404) to come and dine in the Prytaneion, where he will take the seat where Paphlagon used to sit (1404–5). Demos' words of invitation echo the language of an honorary decree (e.g. *IG* i³ 127.37-8 = M-L 94.37-8), appropriately for a citizen, such as Agorakritos, who has benefited the city: the formulaic language would then signify the democracy's approval of Agorakritos' reward. Demos escorts Agorakritos himself, after giving him a luxurious robe (Gk. *batrakhis*) to wear (1406), so Agorakritos, too, has been re-clothed, transformed from humble sausage-seller into civic honorand (since the *batrakhis* was a long garment, it will have covered the actor's grotesque comic costume).

In a final insult, Demos orders Paphlagon to be brought from the house ready to take up his new trade (1407), so that the foreigners (i.e. representatives of Athens' allies), whom he exploited and treated with contempt, will see his humiliation (1408). The point is that at the Lenaea delegations from Athens' allied states were not present in the theatre (as they were at the Dionysia), so Paphlagon's reckoning with rest of the Athenian Empire awaits offstage. This is a variant of the joke made in *Acharnians* (502–6) about slandering the city (or upsetting Cleon) in front of non-Athenians. Paphlagon is probably marched off stage-left, in the direction of the gates where Agorakritos once sold sausages. If the Prytaneion was located to the east of the acropolis, as is widely believed, Demos will accompany Agorakritos out of the theatre in the opposite direction, along the street of tripods, where winning *khorēgoi* dedicated monuments to their victories – a potent symbol of Agorakritos' dramatic success (for a map, see Figure 1).

At the close of the play, Demos seems to have rediscovered the aristocratic virtues of the traditional elite, which have long remained dormant in ordinary Athenians like Agorakritos. Paphlagon, on the other hand, an elite Athenian who built a demagogic career styling himself as a man of the people, has been sentenced to lead the life of a humble sausage-seller. The play's resolution of the problem with which it began (i.e. the domination and corruption of Demos by his own slave, Paphlagon) is the fantasy of a demos with elite values, one that rejects demagogues like Cleon, who serve only its short-term interests but neglect what would keep Athens great (cf. MacDowell 1995: 104–7; Wohl 2002: 78, 108).

But is this convincing? Demos has invited Agorakritos to dine in the Prytaneion, sitting in the very seat where Paphlagon used to sit (1405). And he has magnificently clothed him. Does Agorakritos now look like a scapegoat, fed and maintained at public expense only to be cast out of the city in a ritual expulsion? Is he being duped into becoming the latest *pharmakos* – the favoured politician who will abuse his power and steal from the people until he, in his turn, is driven from the city (cf. Brock 1986; Hesk 2000a: 289–91; Hesk 2000b: 248–61)?

Exodos

The final structural element of a Greek comic drama is the exodos, in which the chorus chant or sing verses as they exit the theatre. This feature is absent from *Cavalry*, and since almost all Aristophanes' plays close with a choral exodos, it is not unlikely that the final words of *Cavalry* have been lost.

In some cases, the action leading up to the exodos is elaborate, as in *Wasps* (1516–37), where the chorus sing to accompany a troupe of dancers, or *Peace* (1329–59), where the chorus and Trygaios sing as the latter is carried offstage. But the exodos is essentially an announcement from the chorus that the play is over. The baldest example is found in *Clouds* (1510–11); however, that play is an incompletely revised version that was probably never staged, so it is impossible to be sure that Aristophanes would have ended a performance so abruptly. Examples of the form of the exodos that are likely to be more typical include a prayer (*Women at the Thesmophoria* 1227–31), songs of triumph (*Birds* 1763–5; *Assembly Women* 1180–3), or a promise that the chorus will sing something more as they leave the stage (cf. *Acharnians* 1232–4; *Wealth* 1209) – probably a traditional or popular song rather than one composed by the poet, which was therefore not included in the text.

The more unusual cases are where the last lines of the play are not given to the chorus (*Cavalry*, *Peace* and *Lysistrata*), and where the chorus has the final word but does not introduce a song (*Frogs*). In *Peace*, it is arguable that the final lines (1363–7), assigned to Trygaios, should belong to the chorus. In *Lysistrata* (1320–1), the actor's lyrics invite the chorus to sing, making it possible that a choral song has been omitted from the manuscripts. Similarly, in *Frogs* (1528–33) a short exodos, perhaps introducing a traditional song, could have been lost.

The ending of *Cavalry* is peculiar because the chorus has said nothing for over seventy lines (cf. 1334). It seems unlikely that they left the stage in silence. Perhaps they announced and sang a traditional song, such as a paean, and the verses introducing it have been lost. Or perhaps the silence of the chorus here is intentional, shifting the expected focus from them to Paphlagon, who is being marched offstage to face his punishment, perhaps to the shouts and hisses of the audience. In that case, it would be plausible for the chorus to burst into spontaneous song once Paphlagon has been led away.

Given the evidence for the form of the comic exodos elsewhere in Aristophanes, it is unlikely that much, if any, material written by

Aristophanes has been lost from the ending of *Cavalry*, or that whatever happened after verse 1408 in the original performance would change our understanding of the play substantially. But the latter is not impossible, and we can only imagine what the Athenians watched in 424 BCE as Aristophanes' prize-winning performance concluded.[5]

9

Modern Reception and Performance

Despite the success of the original performance of *Cavalry* in 424 BCE – arguably Aristophanes' greatest triumph at that time, given that it was the first production he had both written and directed – in more recent times the play has not found much favour or many stages. Nearly a century ago, Gilbert Norwood judged it 'a bad and stupid play', finding fault with its 'unremitting rancour' (1931: 207, 210), and it appears many have shared his view. Professional and amateur productions of *Cavalry* have been few and reception scholarship on them is thin.

The greatest concentration of professional productions have been in Greece, but even there the play has languished in unpopularity: '*Knights* and *Wasps* have seen the fewest modern Greek productions, not just during the annual festival seasons but in more than a century of Aristophanic stage reception generally' (Van Steen 2000: 229). However, during 'Greek national elections ... usually there appears everywhere a politicized Aristophanes, who absorbs and punctures electoral rhetoric with remarkable ease' (ibid. 213–14). In two notable cases, *Cavalry* has been the chosen text. The play was directed by Vyron Tsampoulas in 1974, shortly after the end of military government (1967–1974). The production contained a rewritten parabasis criticizing the recent dictatorship (ibid. 211). In 1989 there was a production directed by Diagoras Chronopoulos at Epidauros. The performance cast Andreas Papandreou (leader of the socialist party PASOK) as Paphlagon, ripe for defeat by Konstantinos Mitsotakis, the leader of the right-wing New Democracy party (ibid. 213–14). Dionyses Kalos, playing Paphlagon, successfully 'ridiculed Andreas Papandreou by imitating his voice and vocabulary' (ibid. 256).

An earlier Greek-directed production, by Stauros Douphexes, was staged in Germany, shortly after the Greek military coup, under the title

'Reiter' ('Riders'). In a rare case of thick description, the performance is well documented by Trilse (1979: 216–24; cf. Flashar 1991: 211–12 with pl. 19, a photograph of the chorus; Van Steen 2000: 256). Douphexes understood that the greatest challenge in adapting *Cavalry* to the modern stage is to find a new identity for the chorus. His production opened in October 1967 with a chorus of fourteen long-haired hippies, 'unemployed samurais' riding hobby-horses and dancing to contemporary beat music. The play made the defence of democracy against demagogues its central theme: Paphlagon was characterized with aspects of Georgios Papadopoulos and Stylianos Pattakos, the central figures of the Greek junta, and the play also alluded to Germany's National Socialist past.

A very different tradition has seen amateur performances of *Cavalry* in ancient Greek in universities, notably in Oxford. Unfortunately, reviews of the best-known production, by the Oxford University Dramatic Society in 1897, are notable for dissatisfaction with the play compared to other closely contemporary Oxford performances (e.g. *Frogs* in 1892). Reviewers were disappointed by the musical score – an important aspect of the reperformance of the original ancient Greek text, since it provided, more than anything else, the opportunity for imaginative modernization – and the large number of errors in the actors' pronunciation of ancient Greek (Wrigley 2011: 76–7).

A much more recent university production captured, however, the political potential of adapting *Cavalry* in translation on the contemporary stage. Brittany Johnson's 'The 2016 Election is Literally Aristophanes' *Knights*' was performed at Barnard College in New York City on the eve of the American Presidential election that brought Donald Trump to office. The play, reviewed by classicist James Romm in the *New Yorker* (October 12, 2016: https://www.newyorker.com/culture/culture-desk /trump-versus-clinton-according-to-aristophanes), included a chorus of failed Republican Presidential candidates, led by Chris Christie and Ben Carson; Donald Trump as Agorakritos, campaigning with the slogan 'Make Athens Great Again'; Hillary Clinton (or 'Hillary Cleon') as Paphlagon; and Demos as a crowd of female newscasters finding a new champion in Trump.

Notes

1 Aristophanes and Drama in Classical Athens

1 For reasons of space, this chapter offers only a very brief general overview of the subject. For more detailed discussion of the many sources behind the information given here, full citation of which would be impractical, see the recommendations in the guide to Further Reading.
2 The Dionysia victory of *Babylonians* in 426 is uncertain but is supported by the likely restoration of Aristophanes' name in the inscription known as the Victors Lists (*IG* ii².2325C.24 with Millis and Olson 2012: 157–8).

2 Aristophanes' *Cavalry* and Cleon

1 Cleon is the only man, until Iphicrates in 371/0, known to have been honoured with permanent dining in the Prytaneion due to military success (see Sommerstein 2001: 242). But he was surely not the only Athenian to receive such an award in the fifth century. The outrage expressed by Aristophanes over it is, therefore, not because it was unprecedented but because it was Cleon who won it. For the reasons for grants of *sitēsis*, see Osborne 1981: 153–70. A late third-century law (*IG* ii² 832.12–17) formalizes who was eligible for permanent dining rights by decree of the assembly: men who set up a trophy (i.e. for a military victory), who restore freedom, who use their private wealth to protect the city, or who are civic benefactors or good advisors. It is possible that similar rules were in place in the fifth century.
2 See Rood 1998: 26–31, with further literature.
3 The text of *Cavalry* provides no further information about Paphlagon's mask. Cratinus (fr. 228 Storey) says that Cleon's face was fearsome and refers to apparently prominent eyebrows. For discussion, see Welsh 1979: 214–15. On portrait masks in Old Comedy, see Dover 1987: 267–74; for doubts about the practicalities, see Marshall 1999. Sommerstein 2001: 242 argues that the absence of a portrait mask in *Cavalry* 231–3 shows that portrait masks were usual in the comic theatre.

4 Hermippus (fr. 47 Storey), dating no later than spring 429, shows that Cleon was already a prominent political figure before the death of Pericles.

5 Cleon inherited the tannery from his father (Σ *Cavalry* 44). Cleon is repeatedly connected with leather in Aristophanes' early plays: apart from *Cavalry*, see *Acharnians* 299–302; *Clouds* 581; *Peace* 270, 648, 753. Other comic poets who ridiculed Cleon do not seem to have joked about him like this; one exception, if it is not a fragment of Aristophanes, is Adespota fr. 297 Storey, where Cleon is called (Gk.) *bursokappos*, probably meaning 'leather-seller'.

6 For Cleon's date of birth, his family and children, see *APF* pp. 319–20 with Table II.

7 The status of Cleon's command at Pylos in 425/4 is the subject of some hesitancy because Thucydides' account of the Pylos campaign does not clearly designate him as *stratēgos*: see Develin 1989: 130; Fornara 1971: 59. Cleon was certainly elected *stratēgos* in the three subsequent years down to his death (424/3, 423/2 and 422/1).

8 Pay for jury service had been introduced by Pericles ([Aristotle] *Athenian Constitution* 27.4), probably in the 450s. Cleon increased it from two to three obols a day, roughly aligning jury pay with the earnings of an unskilled labourer. See Markle 1985.

9 The tribute reassessment (*IG* i³ 71 = M-L 69) was proposed by Thoudippos, who was probably Cleon's son-in-law.

10 *IG* ii² 2318.143-4. For the text and the dates of the performances recorded in this fragment (fr. *a*) of the document known as the Fasti, see Millis and Olson 2012: 8. The date of Kleainetos' dithyrambic *khorēgia* used to be assigned confidently to the year 460/59 BCE; Millis and Olson are more cautious, noting that Kleainetos' victory must date to after 459 but probably before 440 given his likely age.

11 A fragment of Critias (D-K 88 B45 = Aelian, *Historical Miscellany* 10.17), an Athenian contemporary of Cleon's, records that on his death, Cleon left an estate worth 50 talents (i.e. 300,000 drachmas), a huge fortune.

12 For the hostility to Cleon of comic poets other than Aristophanes, the clearest example is Eupolis: 'Cleon, you were the first to tell us to rejoice while doing the city great harm' (fr. 331 Storey); cf. the obviously sarcastic fr. 316 Storey. Another jibe is found in *Comic Adespota* fr.461 Storey

('Cleon is a Prometheus after the fact!'), probably meaning that Cleon claimed to have foreseen events after they had happened.

13 Thucydides was exiled for failing to rescue Amphipolis in 424/3 (Thucydides 5.26.5, cf. 4.104.4-107.2). The suggestion that Cleon might have had a hand in Thucydides' sentence of exile rests only on the fact that Cleon was at this point Athens' most influential demagogue.

14 One possible early political action of Cleon's is the prosecution of Anaxagoras for impiety (Diogenes Laertius 2.3). The trial, probably to be dated to the 430s, would have been a political move against Pericles, who was a friend of Anaxagoras. In 430, Pericles was stripped of his generalship, possibly by Cleon (Plutarch, *Pericles* 35.4).

15 For Cleon's influence with the people, cf. Thucydides 4.21.3.

16 For (Gk.) *perizōsamenos* meaning 'wearing a tradesman's belt', cf. *Birds* 1148 with Dunbar 1998: 411. It is also possible that it means 'wearing an apron' (LSJ *s.v.*). The meaning of the word in this passage has been very widely understood to mean that Cleon simply hitched up his tunic while speaking. But the point of the word is to describe *how* he hitched up his tunic: that is, by wearing a belt so addressing the assembly in his work dress from the tannery, a powerful symbol of his affiliation to the mass of poor Athenian tradespeople. For more on Cleon's eccentric conduct in the assembly, see Plutarch, *Nicias* 7.5, 8.3; *Moralia* 799d.

17 For discussion of 'demagogue comedy', see Sommerstein 2000. Eupolis' *Maricas* was probably performed at the Lenaea in 422/1 (Σ *Clouds* 553). The title of Hermippus' play, *Bakery-Women*, is recorded in Σ *Clouds* 557; it was presumably staged in 421/0 or 420/19. Another demagogue comedy, Plato's *Peisander*, may have followed soon after *Cavalry* (Sommerstein 2000: 439–40).

18 Σ *Acharnians* 378. Aristophanes fr. 71 Henderson, from *Babylonians* (426 BCE), shows that the play cast representatives of the cities of Athens' empire as slaves toiling in a mill. If Cleon did prosecute Aristophanes over *Babylonians*, the accusation might have been inciting revolt among the allied states. Note that in *Cavalry*, Paphlagon's first speech includes a ludicrous accusation of inciting a rebellion in Chalcidice (237-8).

19 On *Wasps* 1284-91, see Biles and Olson 2015: 455-6; Sommerstein 1983: 233-4; Storey 1995.

20 For the evidence and a discussion leading to the conclusion that Cleon at least threatened, and probably took, legal action against Aristophanes, see Sommerstein 2004; Atkinson 1992: 56–61.

21 Instances of the verb (Gk.) *misein* ('to hate') are not widespread in Aristophanes. The largest number in any single play are clustered in *Cavalry* (226, 400, 510, 765, 1020; cf. *Ach.* 299–300, 509; *Clouds* 991, 1225; *Wasps* 1026; *Peace* 501; *Birds* 36, 1547; *Lysistrata* 817, 1018; *Frogs* 1427, 1456; *Assembly Women* 502, 580; *Wealth* 1072). Moreover, Cleon is the only historical individual who is said to be hated in Aristophanes' surviving plays (*Acharnians* 299–300; *Cavalry* 226, 400, 510–11), except (tongue-in-cheek) the general Lamachus at *Peace* 304 (cf. *Acharnians* 1208) and Euripides at *Women at the Thesmophoria* 470. The noun (Gk.) *misos* (hatred) is found with reference to Paphlagon at *Cavalry* 1020 (otherwise it only appears in *Lysistrata* 792, 814). The tragic word (Gk.) *stugein* ('to hate') is not common in Aristophanes and is found only in paratragic or lyric passages (*Acharnians* 33, 472; *Women at the Thesmophoria* 1144; cf. Olson 2002: 77 on *Acharnians* 33).

22 The evidence is a sacrificial stone table on which are inscribed sixteen names. Among these are three men who were probably connected to Aristophanes: Simon, who is named as Priest of Heracles, may be the same man who is one of the leaders of the chorus in *Cavalry* (242); Philonides, who frequently acted as director for Aristophanes; and Amphitheos, who perhaps is to be identified with the character in *Acharnians*.

23 Aristotle mentions this because the children's response creates a rhythmic pattern (trochaics) with the effect of a jingle. Aristotle cautions students of the *Rhetoric* to be careful to avoid such metrical structures in prose and ordinary speech because they are easy to make fun of.

3 *Cavalry* 1–302: Prologue and Parodos

1 Heath 1997: 232–3 collects Aristophanes' accusations against Paphlagon / Cleon in *Cavalry* and shows that each is also found in the orators Aeschines and Demosthenes. See also MacDowell 1993.

2 For the imagery of Paphlagon's political disturbance, see Chapter 5. On the demagogic voice in *Cavalry*, see Hall 2019.

3 The Demosthenes in *Cavalry* was an Athenian military commander of
the second half of the fifth century. We hear of him first in 426 BCE
(Thucydides 3.91.1); he died in 413 in Sicily (Thucydides 7.86.2). In
425/4 he captured Pylos in the western Peloponnese in the action that
Cleon later joined. Nicias was a prominent Athenian general for many
years down to his death in Sicily in 413. He was a supporter of peace
with Sparta and the architect of a peace treaty in 421 (often named after
him as the 'Peace of Nicias'). For Nicias' avoidance of conflict and
preference for peace, see Thucydides 5.16.1; for his fear and caution, e.g.
Thucydides 6.33.3; for his religiosity and superstitious nature,
Thucydides 7.50.4.

4 See Sommerstein 1980: 46–7. Demosthenes and Nicias are identified by
the scholiasts on *Cavalry*: for Demosthenes, see Σ 1; for Demosthenes and
Nicias, see Argumentum A3 and the Dramatis Personae. Note that the
scholia refer to Paphlagon as 'Cleon' throughout (cf. Σ 2). Using the names
Demosthenes and Nicias is clearer and less confusing than using the
designations 'First Slave' and 'Second Slave'. For a different view, see
Henderson 2003a. It must be remembered that from the audience's
perspective, not even the identification of Paphlagon with Cleon is ever
made explicit; for the comic potential this creates, see Osborne 2020:
27–30.

5 The only parallel in Aristophanes for a full iambic line of noises is *Wealth*
895. The verb *kinuresthai* is only otherwise found in classical Greek in
Aeschylus in lyric passages: *Seven against Thebes* 123; *Net Haulers* fr.
47a.804 Sommerstein.

6 The trade of 'sausage-seller' should probably be understood more
accurately as selling 'blood-pudding': see Wilkins 2000: 181 with n. 142.

7 Note that Nicias and Demosthenes, too, set out to find (Gk.) *sōteria* for
themselves (Gk. *nōin*, 12) not for their master (i.e. the people). This is the
first of many red-herrings misdirecting the audience about the surprise
ending of the play, where not only is Paphlagon defeated but Demos
himself is restored to his former, better self. Agorakritos is the only
character who understands that the people need saving from themselves.

8 See Olson 2002: 196–7; Austin and Olson 2004: 177.

9 If Nicias was known for stammering, this would be another way in which
he is recognized by the audience. More than one famous Athenian was

known to have had a speech defect: the politicians Demosthenes
(Plutarch, *Demosthenes* 11.1) and Alcibiades had a lisp (*Wasps* 44–5;
Plutarch, *Alcibiades* 1.4).

10 For audience reactions to ancient Greek drama, see Csapo and Slater
1994: 290.

11 The tricolon is further emphasized by the elisions at the end of each verb
(Gk. *ēikall', ethōpeu', ekolakeu'*). For the theme and vocabulary of flattery,
see Edwards 2010 esp. 322–4, 337; Scholtz 2004: 274–9.

12 Themistocles looms large in the play as an exemplar of democratic
leadership; both Paphlagon and Agorakritos align themselves with him:
see Anderson 1989.

13 For prayers to Zeus the Saviour, cf. Philochorus *FGrH* 328 F5. The
suggestion that Demosthenes drinks the libation that should have
been poured to the Good Spirit is made by the scholiasts (Σ 108).

14 There was an elevated stage in the theatre of Dionysus by this time:
Acharnians 732; cf. *Wasps* 1341, 1514; Csapo 2010: 25–6.

15 For discussion of the number of actors in Old Comedy, see Marshall 2013.

16 Knox 1956 argues for a date of 425, partly on the evidence of echoes in
Cavalry. For a recent discussion of *Cavalry* and *Oedipus Tyrannus*, see
Nelson 2016: 177–203.

17 On the comic body, see Compton-Engle 2015: esp. 17–28. For more
discussion of the vase (Figure 2), see Marshall 2001.

18 According to Thucydides, the slur of not being 'real men' was used by
Cleon against Nicias and the other military commanders in Athens at the
time of the Pylos campaign (Thucydides 4.27.5). Bowie 1993: 45–58 reads
the development of Agorakritos from youth to man as influenced by
Greek myths of maturation; he argues, further, that the plot of *Cavalry*, as
a restoration of order and an end of chaos, is shaped by Athenian rituals,
and their associated myths, that mark the end of the old year and the
beginning of the new (ibid. 66–74).

19 For the political charge of the terms *khrēstos and ponēros* in
contemporary thinking about democracy, see Osborne 2020: 32–3.

20 Cleon's presence in the theatre is implied by a 'deictic' pronoun (Gk.
houtosi), indicating something that can be pointed out (see Chapter 7).

21 For portrait masks, see Chapter 2.

22 Euboea was strategically vital to Athens because it was the largest and
closest island where herd animals could be kept safe from Peloponnesian

invasions of Attica (Thucydides 2.14.1; cf. 7.28.1). Euboea had a history of revolt from Athens (Thucydides 1.114.1; cf. 8.95.7-96.1).

23 Simon might be the same man who wrote a manual on horsemanship (cf. Xenophon, *Cavalry Commander* 1.1). No cavalry commander named Panaitios can be identified.

24 See Christ 1998: 48–71; Todd 1993: 92–4; and the debate between Osborne 1990 and Harvey 1990.

4 *Cavalry* 303–610: First Agon and Parabasis

1 The rarity of *anaideia* extends to its cognates: forms of the adjective *anaidēs* are found three times in *Cavalry* (385 twice, 638) and twice in *Lysistrata* (369, 1015); the adverb *anaidōs* appears once in *Women at the Thesmophoria* (525). The importance of the concept in *Cavalry* is underlined by the appearance of the verbs *anaideuomai* (397) and *hyperanaideuomai* (1206), apparently meaning, respectively, 'continue to be outrageous' and 'be surpassed in outrageousness'. They are found nowhere else in classical Greek and may be Aristophanic coinages.

2 Compare the range of meaning in its antonym *aidōs*: respect, self-respect, honour, shame, compassion, forgiveness etc. (cf. LSJ *s.v.* I; Cairns 1993).

3 On the concept of *sōphrosynē* in ancient Greek culture, see North 1966; Rademaker 2005 (esp. 76–92 for its aristocratic overtones).

4 The translation of *kasalbasō* (355) as 'I'll cuss out' is tentative. Usually it has been translated 'I'll screw the generals' (i.e. like whores): e.g. Henderson 1998: 275; Sommerstein 1981: 45; Anderson and Dix 2020: 114. The root, *kasalb-* is pre-Greek, and the noun *kasalbas* (cf. *Assembly Women* 1106) is vulgar (Beekes *s.v.*); like *pornē*, *kasalbas* clearly means 'whore'. The verb *kasalbazein* is extremely rare and its meaning is uncertain. A notice in the scholia (*Cavalry* Σ 355) interprets it as 'I'll hurl abuse' (i.e. like a *kasalbas*), which would explain the element *-bazō* ('talk'): insults rather than sexual activity may be the true sense here (cf. LSJ *s.v.*). Note that in Thucydides' narrative of the Pylos campaign (4.27.5), Cleon insults Nicias in assembly.

5   For the unusual word, not found elsewhere in comedy, meaning 'being lumpy' (i.e. having cysts), see LSJ *s.v. khalaza*; Aristotle, *Generation of Animals* 603b18.

6   Simonides fr. 7 Campbell quoted in Σ 405, where it is noted that the verse is drawn from Simonides' poems written for victories in chariot racing, fittingly for the equestrian character of the chorus.

7   For Cleon's possible connection to Harmodios, see *APF* pp.145, 320, 476–7; for doubts, Bourriot 1982: 418–30. For recent discussion, see Saldutti 2014: 39–46.

8   On the importance of the role of *koryphaios* in comedy, see Henderson 2013: 288.

9   See *Banqueters* T3 Henderson; *Babylonians* T1 Henderson; and *Acharnians: Hypothesis* 1.32 (Olson 2002: 1).

10 For a summary of the evidence for Magnes' career, see Storey vol. 2, pp. 338–9 (with further literature). Magnes' victories are recorded in the inscriptions known as the Victors Lists (*IG* ii^2 2325.44; Millis and Olson 2012: 163): see Storey vol. 2, p. 342.

11 Nothing more is known about this play: see Storey vol. 1, p. 385.

12 For Cratinus' career, see Storey vol. 1, pp. 234–9 (with further literature). Cratinus ridicules Konnos in fr. 349 Storey. More information on Konnos is found in Sommerstein 1981: 172 and Anderson and Dix 2020: 134. For Cratinus' love of wine, see Cratinus T1 Storey. He mentions his drunkenness more than once in *Wineskin*: frr. 199, 203 Storey. For discussion of the evidence for *Wineskin*, see Storey vol. 1, pp. 362–5. For *Wineskin* as a response to Aristophanes' *Cavalry*, see Cratinus T3 Storey. For Cratinus' victory with *Wineskin* over Aristophanes' *Clouds*, see Cratinus T9c Storey.

13 For the little that is known about Crates' career, see Storey vol. 1, pp. 200–1.

14 The expression 'eleven oars' has never been certainly explained. It is of note that the scholiasts (Σ 546) do not understand it, and they may be correct in thinking that it is nautical terminology that would have been familiar to many in the original audience. For different suggestions and further literature, see Hubbard 1990; Lech 2009.

15 Among Phormion's exploits was the memorable defeat of a Peloponnesian fleet much larger than his own in 429/8 BCE (Thucydides 2.83-4). His

popularity is suggested, too, by Aristophanes' attitude: although he pokes fun at Phormion as a formidably tough and hirsute fighter (*Peace* 348, *Lysistrata* 804; cf. Eupolis fr. 268 Storey, where he is called 'Ares', i.e. the god of war), his words are not as hostile as they are towards many notable Athenians.

16 For a different interpretation (Theoros trying to make fun of his and Cleon's enemies, the cavalry), see Halliwell 1982: 153.

5 *Cavalry* 611–996: Report of Off-Stage Action and Second Agon

1 The words *elasibrontos* ('thunderous') and *anarrēgnumi* ('burst forth', or 'blurt'), used metaphorically of speech, are only otherwise known from Pindar, frr. 144 Snell-Maehler; 180 Race.

2 Surprising as the phrase 'look mustard' may seem in English, such expressions are quite widely found in Aristophanes: see Olson 2002: 144.

3 For a different view, see Scholtz 2004: esp. 265–71, who argues that speaking of 'love for the demos' is an accusation of specious rhetoric levelled at rivals (e.g. Isocrates 8.121) rather than a real strategy employed by speakers to win over their audience.

4 For a revisionist discussion drawing attention to the problems in the standard account, see Osborne 2018 with further literature.

5 For further discussion of *khaskein* in *Cavalry*, especially its sexual implications, see Wohl 2002: 80–92.

6 For echoes of *Prometheus Bound* in *Cavalry*, see Flintoff 1983: 1 n. 3.

7 For 'Themistocles' career, see Podlecki 1975.

8 This is a suggestion made by Sommerstein 1981: 189. Hornblower vol. 1, p. 426 notes that Mytilenean emissaries were in Athens at the time of Cleon's speech (Thucydides 3.36.5, 49.2), making his accusations of bribery more plausible.

9 See Lippman, Schahill and Schultz 2006. Earlier in the action at Pylos, Demosthenes had captured the shield of the famed Spartan commander Brasidas (Thucydides 4.12.1).

10 On silphium, see Anderson and Dix 2020: 175–6.

11 In 924 the unusual word *ipoumenos* ('crushed') perhaps contains a third
    echo of *Prometheus Bound* (365). If so, Agorakritos is here likened to
    Prometheus buried beneath Mount Etna, suggesting that his battle with
    Paphlagon is not yet over.

12 A similar metatheatrical joke appears in *Clouds* (1036), where the Unjust
    Argument responds to the long pnigos delivered by the Just Argument
    and the chorus (1009–33), saying that he has been choking (*pnigesthai*)
    for some time in eagerness to speak.

6 *Cavalry* 997–1150: Divination Contest and Duet

1 In addition to Bacis, oracle collections are attested in fifth-century
   evidence for the following: the Sibyl: Aristophanes, *Peace* 1095 (cf.
   Heraclitus fr. 92 D-K); Orpheus: Aristophanes, *Frogs* 1032–3; Musaeus:
   Herodotus 7.6.3-5, 8.96, 9.43 (cf. Plato, *Republic* 364e for books of
   'Orpheus and Musaeus'); Laius: Herodotus 5.43. Note also Lysistratos in
   Herodotus 8.96, though it is unclear whether he was a prophet or merely
   a chresmologue. For oracle collections for which the evidence is of later
   date, see Fontenrose 1978: 158–65.

2 A point made well by Parker 1985: 302: '... clients of diviners are by no
   means unreservedly credulous. They are often suspicious or openly
   contemptuous of particular forms of divination or individual diviners ...
   Such scepticism supports rather than subverts belief in the possibility of
   divination, since failures can be explained through the incompetence or
   fraud of particular diviners. The society that abuses diviners is the society
   that consults them.'

3 In Greek, the name *Kleōn* sounds like the word for a dog, *kuōn*. The pun
   plays a much larger role in Aristophanes' play *Wasps* (422 BCE), in which
   a dog representing Cleon is put on trial. It is possible that Cleon had
   characterized himself as Athens' guard dog, or perhaps it was a nickname
   that he had acquired.

4 Agorakritos' reinterpretation of the oracle rests on a pun, in Greek,
   linking Paphlagon with Antileon, a long-dead tyrant of Chalcis (Aristotle,
   Politics 1316a29-32). The idea behind the stocks, an instrument of public

punishment, is inspired by the words 'iron' and 'wood', the materials from which the stocks would be constructed.

5 It is not clear how far the quotation from the *Little Iliad* (fr. 2 West) runs. Line 1056 is certainly quotation, but Σ 1056 includes the first half of 1057 in addition.

6 Σ 1069 explains that Philostratos was a 'pimp who wore makeup' (or otherwise dressed extravagantly). *Lysistrata* 954–8 confirms that there was an Athenian pimp known as Fox-Dog.

7 Extrametrical speech is quite widely found in Aristophanes, but it is uncommon enough that it must have made an impression on the audience. There are only two instances in Aristophanes of the extrametrical use of the particle (Gk.) *eien*, both in *Cavalry*. The second example (1238) occurs after Paphlagon's first question in the interrogation that will lead to the discovery of Agorakritos' identity and clearly highlights what is an ominous and momentous turning point in the plot. Demos' remark here (1078) should indicate a significant pause.

8 For Diopeithes' decree, see Plutarch, *Pericles* 32.1. Telecleides fr. 7 Storey says that he was 'somewhat crazy'. Phrynichus fr. 9 Storey suggests that he was given to ecstatic ritual dancing. Ameipsias fr. 10 Storey says that 'some people invent oracles and give them to the lunatic Diopeithes to recite'. He is mentioned again by Aristophanes in *Wasps* (380), with a pun on his name (which means 'Trust in Zeus') that might suggest overly optimistic reliance on the gods.

9 For discussion of the thematic significance of these dreams, see Anderson 1991.

10 The verb *gerontagōgein* ('tend to an old man') appears in Sophocles fr. 487 Lloyd-Jones and in an unknown comic poet (Adespota fr. 740 *PCG*). Here, it means 'educate an old man', by analogy with the more familiar *paidagōgein* ('educate a child'). It no doubt also put the audience in mind of *dēmagōgein* (demagoguery).

11 In Thucydides (2.63.2), Pericles likens Athens to a tyrant over the empire, and Cleon describes the empire as an actual tyranny (3.37.2). For discussion, see Tuplin 1985. For Demos as a tyrant in this passage of *Cavalry*, see Edwards 2010: 325–7. On tyranny in Old Comedy, see Henderson 2003b.

12 In Thucydides, Cleon criticizes the Athenians for wanting to appear clever when they would do better to obey the laws and not overestimate their

abilities (3.37.3-4, 3.38.6). The image of vomiting up ill-gotten gains is memorably applied to Cleon in *Acharnians* (6).

13   There has been much discussion over whether Aristophanes allows Demos to save face here or deepens his criticisms of democracy. See Reinders 2001: 170–8, 191–2.

7 *Cavalry* 1151–1315: Competition in Public Service and Second Parabasis

1   There are numerous echoes in the Greek text. The verb *episkopei* ('watches over') in *Cavalry* 1173 echoes the noun *episkopos* ('guardian') in Solon fr. 4.3 Gerber; the phrase *hyperekhei sou khytran* (*Cavalry* 1174) echoes *kheiras hyperthen ekhei* ('holds her hands above') in 4.4; and Agorakritos' subsequent use (1178) of the epithet of Athene 'daughter of the almighty father' (Gk. *obrimopatra*) reflects 4.3.

2   For the relationship of *Maricas* and *Cavalry*, see Heath 1990; Storey 1993.

3   Euripides' *Telephus* is a favourite of Aristophanes, parodied extensively in *Acharnians* and *Women at the Thesmophoria*: see Olson 2002: lviii-lxi; Austin and Olson 2004: lvi-lviii.

4   For discussion of Aristophanes' use of *Bellerophon*, which is parodied extensively in *Peace*, see Olson 1998: xxxii-xxxiv.

5   The translation 'Mouthenians' is borrowed from Sommerstein 1981: 127.

6   For more information on the family of Carcinus, see Sommerstein 1983: 246.

7   For a statement of this view, see Timaeus (*FGrH* 566 F 152): '[Timaeus writes that] poets make clear their own natures.' Cf. *Acharnians* 410–13, where Euripides goes about in rags because he writes tragedies including beggars; and *Women at the Thesmophoria* 167, where Agathon says that poetry necessarily reflects a poet's nature.

8 *Cavalry* 1316–1408: Closing Episodes and Exodos

1   For the fame of Miltiades, see Herodotus 6.132-6; Plutarch, *Cimon* 4.3. For Aristides 'the Just', see Plutarch, *Aristides* 26.1, 27.1; Demosthenes 23.209.

2 Edmunds 1987b: 256–63 argues Demos is still an old man but beautified in the fashion of the era of the Persian Wars, to which Athens will now return; but Olson 1990 argues persuasively that he has indeed become young (cf. Stone 1984: 403 suggesting that Demos wears the mask of a young man).

3 For the rituals at the Athenian Thargelia, see Parker 2005: 481–3; for the *pharmakos* in Greek culture, see Bremmer 1983; Burkert 1985: 82–4.

4 The plot of *Cavalry* has been analyzed as a dramatization of the 'scapegoat complex', with Paphlagon driven out of the city as a scapegoat to bring about community purification and renewal: see Bennett and Tyrell 1990: esp. 236; cf. Bowie 1993: 74–5.

5 For discussion of the various difficulties in the ending of *Cavalry*, see Harder 1997.

References

Anderson, C. A. 1989. 'Themistocles and Cleon in Aristophanes' *Knights* 763ff.' *American Journal of Philology* 110: 10–16.

Anderson, C. A. 1991. 'The Dream-Oracles of Athena, *Knights* 1090–95.' *Transactions of the American Philological Association* 121: 149–55.

Anderson, C. A. 2003. 'The Gossiping Triremes in Aristophanes' *Knights*, 1300–1315.' *Classical Journal* 99: 1–9.

Anderson, C. A. and Dix, T. K. 2020. *A Commentary on Aristophanes'* Knights. Michigan.

Atkinson, J. E. 1992. 'Curbing the Comedians: Cleon versus Aristophanes and Syracosius' Decree.' *Classical Quarterly* 42: 56–64.

Austin, C. and Olson, S. D. 2004. *Aristophanes: Thesmophoriazusae*. Oxford.

Bakola, E. 2010. *Cratinus and the Art of Comedy*. Oxford.

Bearzot, C. 2007. 'Political Murder in Classical Greece.' *Ancient Society* 37: 37–61.

Bennett, L. J. and Tyrell, W. B. 1990. 'Making sense of Aristophanes' *Knights*.' *Arethusa* 23: 235–54.

Biles, Z. P. 2011. *Aristophanes and the Poetics of Competition*. Cambridge.

Biles, Z. P. and Olson, S. D. 2015. *Aristophanes: Wasps*. Oxford.

Bourriot, F. 1982. 'La famille et le milieu social de Cléon.' *Historia* 31: 404–35.

Bowie, A. M. 1993. *Aristophanes: Myth, Ritual and Comedy*. Cambridge.

Bremmer, J. 1983. 'Scapegoat Rituals in Ancient Greece.' *Harvard Studies in Classical Philology* 87: 299–320.

Brock, R. W. 1986. 'The double plot in Aristophanes' *Knights*.' *Greek, Roman, and Byzantine Studies* 27: 15–27.

Bugh, G. R. 1988. *The Horsemen of Athens*. Princeton.

Burkert, W. 1985. *Greek Religion*. Cambidge, MA.

Cairns, D. L. 1993: *Aidōs: The Psychology and Ethics of Honour and Shame in Ancient Greek Literature*. Oxford.

Carawan, E. M. 1990. 'The Five Talents Cleon Coughed Up (Schol. Ar. *Ach.* 6).' *Classical Quarterly* 40: 137–47.

Christ, M. R. 1998. *The Litigious Athenian*. Baltimore.

Compton-Engle, G. 2015. *Costume in the Comedies of Aristophanes*. Cambridge.

Connor, W. R. 1971. *The New Politicians of Fifth-Century Athens*. Princeton.

Csapo, E. 2010. *Actors and Icons of the Ancient Theater*. Chichester.

Csapo, E. and Slater, W. J. 1994. *The Context of Ancient Drama*. Michigan.

Develin, R. 1989. *Athenian Officials, 684–321 BC*. Cambridge.

Dillery, J. 2005. 'Chresmologues and Manteis: Independent Diviners and the Problem of Authority.' In S. I. Johnston and P. Struck (eds) *Mantike: Studies in Ancient Divination*. Leiden: 167–231.

Donlan, W. 1999. *The Aristocratic Ideal in Ancient Greece*.[2] Wauconda, IL.

Dover, K. J. 1972. *Aristophanic Comedy*. London.

Dover, K. J. 1974. *Greek Popular Morality in the Time of Plato and Aristotle*. Oxford.

Dover, K. J. 1978. *Greek Homosexuality*. Cambridge, MA.

Dover, K. J. 1987. *Greek and the Greeks: Collected Papers. Language, Poetry, Drama*. Vol. 1. Oxford.

Dow, S. 1969. 'Some Athenians in Aristophanes.' *American Journal of Archaeology* 73: 234–5.

Dunbar, N. 1998. *Aristophanes: Birds*. Oxford.

Edmunds, L. 1987a. *Cleon, Knights, and Aristophanes' Politics*. Lanham, MD.

Edmunds, L. 1987b. 'The Aristophanic Cleon's "Disturbance" of Athens.' *American Journal of Philology* 108: 233–63.

Edwards, A. T. 2010. 'Tyrants and Flatterers: *Kolakeia* in Aristophanes' *Knights* and *Wasps*.' In P. Mitsis and C. Tsagalis (eds) *Allusion, Authority, and Truth: Critical Perspectives on Greek Poetic and Rhetorical Praxis*. Berlin and New York: 303–38.

Flashar, H. 1991. *Inszenierung der Antike: das griechische Drama auf der Bühne der Neuzeit 1585–1990*. Munich.

Flintoff, E. 1983. 'Aristophanes and the *Prometheus Bound*.' *Classical Quarterly* 33: 1–5.

Fontenrose, J. E. 1978. *The Delphic Oracle: Its Responses and Operations, with a catalogue of responses*. Berkeley.

Fornara, C. W. 1971. *The Athenian Board of Generals from 501 to 404*. Wiesbaden.

Fornara, C. W. 1973. 'Cleon's Attack against the Cavalry.' *Classical Quarterly* 23: 24.

Gelzer, T. 1960. *Der epirrhematische Agon bei Aristophanes*. Munich.

Goldhill, S. 1987. 'The Great Dionysia and Civic Ideology.' *Journal of Hellenic Studies* 107: 58–76.

Gould, J. 1973. '*Hiketeia*.' *Journal of Hellenic Studies* 93: 74–103.

Hall, E. 2018. 'The Boys from Cydathenaeum: Aristophanes versus Cleon Again.' In D. Allen et al. (eds) *How to Do Things with History: New Approaches to Ancient Greece*. Oxford: 339–63.

Hall, E. 2019. 'Competitive Vocal Performance in Aristophanes' *Knights*.' In A. Markantonatos and E. Volonaki (eds) *Poet and Orator: A Symbiotic Relationship in Democratic Athens*. Berlin and Boston: 71–82.

Halliwell, S. 1980. 'Aristophanes' Apprenticeship.' *Classical Quarterly* 30: 33–45.

Halliwell, S. 1982. 'Notes on some Aristophanic jokes (*Ach.* 854–9; *Kn.* 608–10; *Peace* 695–9; *Thesm.* 605; *Frogs* 1039).' *Liverpool Classical Monthly* 7: 153–4.

Halliwell, S. 2022. *Acharnians, Knights, Wasps, Peace: a verse translation with introductions and notes*. Oxford.

Harder, R. E. 1997. 'Der Schluss von Aristophanes' *Rittern*.' *Prometheus* 23: 108–18.

Harvey, D. 1990. 'The Sykophant and Sykophancy: Vexatious Redefinition?' In P. Cartledge et al. (eds) *Nomos: Essays in Athenian Law, Politics and Society*. Cambridge: 103–21.

Heath, M. 1990. 'Aristophanes and his Rivals.' *Greece & Rome* 37: 143–58.

Heath, M. 1997. 'Aristophanes and the Discourse of Politics.' In G. W. Dobrov (ed.) *The City as Comedy: Society and Representation in Athenian Drama*. Chapel Hill: 230–49.

Henderson, J. J. 1991. *The Maculate Muse: Obscene Language in Attic Comedy.*[2] Oxford.

Henderson, J. J. 1998. *Aristophanes: Acharnians, Knights*. Cambridge, MA.

Henderson, J. J. 2003a. 'When an identity was expected: the slaves in Aristophanes' *Knights*.' In G. W. Bakewell and J. P. Sickinger (eds) *Gestures: Essays in Ancient History, Literature, and Philosophy presented to Alan L. Boegehold*. Oxford: 63–73.

Henderson, J. J. 2003b. 'Demos, Demagogue, Tyrant in Attic Old Comedy.' In K. A. Morgan (ed.) *Sovereignty and Its Discontents in Ancient Greece: Popular Tyranny*. Austin: 155–79.

Henderson, J. J. 2013. 'The Comic Chorus and the Demagogue.' In R. Gagné and M. G. Hopman (eds) *Choral Mediations in Greek Tragedy*. Cambridge: 278–96.

Hesk, J. 2000a. *Deception and Democracy in Classical Athens*. Cambridge.

Hesk, J. 2000b. 'Intratext and Irony in Aristophanes.' In A. Sharrock and H. Morales (eds) *Intratextuality: Greek and Roman Textual Relations*. Oxford.

Hesk, J. 2007. 'Combative Capping in Aristophanic Comedy.' *Cambridge Classical Journal* 53: 124–60.

Hornblower, S. 1991–2008. *A Commentary on Thucydides*. 3 vols. Oxford.

Hubbard, T. K. 1990. 'The Knights' Eleven Oars (Aristophanes, *Equites* 546–547).' *Classical Journal* 85: 115–18.

Hubbard, T. K. 1991. *The Mask of Comedy: Aristophanes and the Intertextual Parabasis*. Ithaca.

Hubbard, T. K. 2003. *Homosexuality in Greece and Rome: A Sourcebook of Basic Documents*. Berkeley.

Imperio, O. 2004. *Parabasi di Aristofane*. Bari.

Issacharoff, M. 1981. 'Space and Reference in Drama.' *Poetics Today* 2: 211–24.

Kagan, D. 1974. *The Archidamian War*. Ithaca.

Kloss, G. 2001. *Erscheinungsformen komischen Sprechens bei Aristophanes*. Berlin and New York.

Knox, B. M. W. 1956. 'The Date of the *Oedipus Tyrannus* of Sophocles.' *American Journal of Philology* 77: 133–47.

Kugelmeier, C. 1996. *Reflexe früher und zeitgenössischer Lyrik in der alten attischen Komödie*. Stuttgart

Landfester, M. 1967. *Die Ritter des Aristophanes*. Amsterdam.

Lech, M. L. 2009. 'The Knights' Eleven Oars: In Praise of Phormio? Aristophanes' *Knights* 546–7.' *Classical Journal* 105: 19–26.

Lind, H. 1990. *Der Gerber Kleon in den* Rittern *des Aristophanes: Studien zur Demagogenkömodie*. Frankfurt.

Lippman, M., Scahill, D. and Schultz, P. 2006. '*Knights* 843–59, the Nike Temple Bastion, and Cleon's Shields from Pylos.' *American Journal of Archaeology* 110: 551–63.

Littlefield, D. J. 1968. 'Metaphor and Myth: The Unity of Aristophanes' *Knights*.' *Studies in Philology* 65: 1–22.

MacDowell, D. M. 1993. 'Foreign Birth and Athenian Citizenship in Aristophanes.' In A. H. Sommerstein et al. (eds) *Tragedy, Comedy and the Polis*. Bari: 359–71.

MacDowell, D. M. 1995. *Aristophanes and Athens: An Introduction to the Plays*. Oxford.

Markle, M. M. 1985. 'Jury Pay and Assembly Pay at Athens.' *History of Political Thought* 6: 265–97.

Marr, J. 1995. 'The Death of Themistocles.' *Greece & Rome* 42: 159–67.

Marshall, C. W. 1999. 'Some Fifth-Century Masking Conventions.' *Greece & Rome* 46: 188–202.

Marshall, C. W. 2001. 'A Gander at the Goose Play.' *Theatre Journal* 53: 53–71.

Marshall, C. W. 2013. 'Three Actors in Old Comedy, Again.' In G. M. W. Harrison and V. Liapis (eds) *Performance in Greek and Roman Theatre*. Leiden: 257–78.

Millis, B. and Olson, S. D. 2012. *Inscriptional Records for the Dramatic Festivals in Athens*. Leiden and Boston.

Muecke, F. 1998. 'Oracles in Aristophanes.' *Seminari Romani di Cultura Greca* 1: 257–74.

Nelson, S. A. 2016. *Aristophanes and His Tragic Muse: Comedy, Tragedy and the Polis in 5th Century Athens*. Leiden and Boston.

Newiger, H.-J. 1957. *Metapher und Allegorie: Studien zu Aristophanes*. Munich.

North, H. 1966. *Sophrosyne: Self-Knowledge and Self-Restraint in Greek Literature*. Ithaca.

Norwood, G. 1931. *Greek Comedy*. London.

Olson, S. D. 1990. 'The New Demos of Aristophanes' *Knights*.' *Eranos* 88: 60–3.

Olson, S. D. 1998. *Aristophanes: Peace*. Oxford.

Olson, S. D. 2002. *Aristophanes: Acharnians*. Oxford.

Olson, S. D. 2013. 'Slaves and Politics in Early Aristophanic Comedy.' In B. Akrigg and R. Tordoff (eds) *Slaves and Slavery in Ancient Greek Comic Drama*. Cambridge: 63–75.

Osborne, M. J. 1981. 'Entertainment in the Prytaneion at Athens.' *Zeitschrift für Papyrologie und Epigraphik* 41: 153–70.

Osborne, R. G. 1990. 'Vexatious Litigation in Classical Athens: Sykophancy and the Sykophant.' In P. Cartledge et al. (eds) *Nomos: Essays in Athenian Law, Politics and Society*. Cambridge: 83–102.

Osborne, R. G. 2018. 'Imaginary Intercourse: An Illustrated History of Greek Pederasty.' In D. Allen et al. (eds) *How to Do Things with History: New Approaches to Ancient Greece*. Oxford. 313–38.

Osborne, R. G. 2020. 'Politics and Laughter: The case of Aristophanes' *Knights*.' In R. M. Rosen and H. P. Foley (eds) *Aristophanes and Politics: New Studies*. Leiden and Boston: 24–44.

Parker, L. P. E. 1997. *The Songs of Aristophanes*. Oxford.

Parker, R. C. T. 1985. 'Greek States and Greek Oracles.' In P. Cartledge and D. Harvey (eds) *Crux: Essays in Greek History presented to G. E. M. de Ste. Croix on his 75th birthday. History of Political Thought* 6. Exeter: 298–326.

Parker, R. C. T. 2005. *Polytheism and Society at Athens*. Oxford.

Platter, C. 2007. *Aristophanes and the Carnival of Genres*. Baltimore.

Podlecki, A. 1975. *The Life of Themistocles: A Critical Survey of the Literary and Archaeological Evidence*. Toronto.

Rademaker, A. 2005. *Sophrosyne and the Rhetoric of Self-Restraint*. Mnemosyne Supp. 259. Amsterdam.

Reinders, P. 2001. *Demos Pyknites: Untersuchungen zur Darstellung des Demos in der Alten Komödie*. Stuttgart.

Rood, T. 1998. *Thucydides: Narrative and Explanation*. Oxford.

Roselli, D. K. 2011. *Theater of the People: Spectators and Society in Ancient Athens*. Austin.

Rosen, R. M. 1988. *Old Comedy and the Iambographic Tradition*. Atlanta.

Ruffell, I. 2011. *Politics and Anti-Realism in Athenian Old Comedy: The Art of the Impossible*. Oxford.

Saldutti, V. 2014. *Cleone: un politico ateniese*. Bari.

Scholtz, A. 2004. 'Friends, Lovers, Flatterers: Demophilic Courtship in Aristophanes' *Knights*.' *Transactions of the American Philological Association* 134: 263–93.

Silk, M. S. 2000. *Aristophanes and the Definition of Comedy*. Oxford.

Slater, N. W. 2002. *Spectator Politics: Metatheatre and Performance in Aristophanes*. Philadelphia.

Smith, N. J. 1989. 'Diviners and Divination in Aristophanic Comedy.' *Classical Antiquity* 8: 140–58.

Sommerstein, A. H. 1980. 'Notes on Aristophanes' *Knights*.' *Classical Quarterly* 30: 46–56.

Sommerstein, A. H. 1981. *Knights* (repr. 1997). Warminster.

Sommerstein, A. H. 1983. *Wasps* (repr. 1996). Warminster.

Sommerstein, A. H. 1985. *Peace* (repr. 2005). Warminster.

Sommerstein, A. H. 2000. 'Platon, Eupolis, and the "Demagogue Comedy".' In F. D. Harvey and J. Wilkins (eds) *The Rivals of Aristophanes*. London and Swansea: 437–51.

Sommerstein, A. H. 2001. *Wealth*. Warminster.

Sommerstein, A. H. 2004. 'Harassing the satirist: The alleged attempts to prosecute Aristophanes.' In I. Sluiter and R. M. Rosen (eds) *Free Speech in Classical Antiquity*. Leiden and Boston: 145–74.

Spence, I. G. 1993. *The Cavalry of Classical Greece: A Social and Military History*. Oxford.

Stone, L. M. 1984. *Costume in Aristophanic Comedy*. Salem.

Storey, I. C. 1993. 'Notus est omnibus Eupolis?' In A. H. Sommerstein et al. (eds) *Tragedy, Comedy and the Polis*. Bari: 373–96.

Storey, I. C. 1995. 'Wasps 1284–91 and the Portrait of Kleon in *Wasps*.' *Scholia* 4: 3–23.

Storey, I. C. 2003. *Eupolis, Poet of Old Comedy*. Oxford.

Storey, I. C. and Allan, A. 2005. *A Guide to Ancient Greek Drama*. Oxford.

Stroud, R. S. 1971. 'Greek Inscriptions: Theozotides and the Athenian Orphans.' *Hesperia* 40: 280–301.

Todd, S. C. 1993. *The Shape of Athenian Law*. Oxford.

Totaro, P. 1999. *Le seconde parabasi di Aristofane*. Stuttgart.

Trendall, A. D. and Webster, T. B. L. 1971. *Illustrations of Greek Drama*. London.

Trilse, C. 1979. *Antike und Theater heute*. Berlin.

Tuplin, C. J. 1985. 'Imperial Tyranny: Some Reflections on a Classical Greek Political Metaphor.' In P. Cartledge and D. Harvey (eds) *Crux: Essays in Greek History presented to G. E. M. de Ste. Croix on his 75th birthday. History of Political Thought* 6. Exeter: 348–75.

Tylawsky, E. 2002. *Saturio's Inheritance: The Greek Ancestry of the Roman Comic Parasite*. Oxford and New York.

Van Steen, G. A. H. 2000. *Venom in Verse: Aristophanes in Modern Greece*. Princeton.

Welsh, D. 1979. 'Knights 230–3 and Cleon's Eyebrows.' *Classical Quarterly* 29: 214–15.

Whitman, C. H. 1964. *Aristophanes and the Comic Hero*. Cambridge, MA.

Wilkins, J. 2000. *The Boastful Chef: The Discourse of Food in Ancient Greek Comedy*. Oxford.

Wilson, N. G. 2007a. *Aristophanis Fabulae*. 2 vols. Oxford.

Wilson, N. G. 2007b. *Aristophanea: Studies on the Text of Aristophanes*. Oxford.

Wilson, P. 2000. *The Athenian Institution of the* Khoregia: *The Chorus, the City and the Stage*. Cambridge.

Wohl, V. 2002. *Love Among the Ruins: The Erotics of Democracy in Classical Athens*. Princeton.

Woodhead, A. G. 1960. 'Thucydides' Portrait of Cleon.' *Mnemosyne* 13: 289–317.

Wright, M. 2012. *The Comedian as Critic: Greek Old Comedy and Poetics*. London.

Wrigley, A. 2011. *Performing Greek Drama in Oxford and on Tour with the Balliol Players*. Exeter.

Yu, K. W. 2017. 'The Divination Contest of Calchas and Mopsus and Aristophanes' *Knights*.' *Greek, Roman, and Byzantine Studies* 57: 910–34.

Further Reading

There are several scholarly translations of *Cavalry* available: Henderson 1998; Halliwell 2022; Sommerstein 1981. For readers of the Greek text, for which see Wilson's OCT (2007a), the most recent commentaries are Anderson and Dix 2020 and Sommerstein 1981; both contain much information on all matters, literary, historical and linguistic. For a general introduction to Aristophanes, see MacDowell 1995.

The sources behind the overview of Athenian theatre in Chapter 1 may be found in *DFA* and Csapo and Slater 1994; for discussion, see Roselli 2011. On the organization of choruses, see Wilson 2000. On civic ideology and Athenian drama, see Goldhill 1987. For a fuller general introduction than can be presented in this book, see Storey and Allan 2005: 1–71.

The most complete study of Cleon, the subject of Chapter 2, is Saldutti 2014 (in Italian). On Cleon and other Athenian demagogues, Connor 1971 remains fundamental. For a recent reassessment of Cleon, see Hall 2018. For a full account of the Pylos campaign, see Kagan 1974: 218–59. On the Athenian cavalry, see Bugh 1988 and Spence 1993 (esp. 9–17 for an overview).

Cavalry lacks a dedicated monograph or volume of collected essays, but a number of different studies are fundamental to Chapters 3–8. See Slater 2002: 68–85 for the stage action and dramatic development. Various themes in *Cavalry* have been discussed in detail: see Wilkins 2000: 179–201 on food; Scholtz 2004 and Wohl 2002: 73–123 on erotic rhetoric and sex; Edmunds 1987b on the political imagery of disturbance. On ritual and mythical patterns in *Cavalry*, see Bowie 1993: 45–77; Bennett and Tyrell 1990. The 'divination contest' in Chapter 6 has been discussed recently by Yu 2017, and oracles in

Cavalry are investigated by Ruffell 2011: 65–77. On oracles and diviners in Aristophanes, see also Dillery 2005; Muecke 1998; Smith 1989. The 'surprise' ending to *Cavalry* has been much discussed: see Brock 1986; Hesk 2000b: 248–61. Osborne 2020 looks at *Cavalry* and humour theory.

General Index

acropolis, Athens, *Fig.* 1
  and Athene Polias 51
  and the Erechtheum 61
  and Kydathenaion 19
  monuments on 40, 46
  and the Parthenon 105
  and the Pnyx 28, 74
  and the Propylaea 123
  and the Prytaneion 130
  and the Theatre of Dionysus 1
actors
  costume in Old Comedy 35
  gestures 36, 74, 108–9
  number
    in *Cavalry* 33, 112
    in Old Comedy 1, 140 n.15
    in tragedy 1, 33
  prizes 4–5
  recruitment 4
  roles in *Cavalry* 33, 53, 112
  voice control, in pnigos 41, 83,
    144 n.12
Aeschines, Athenian politician and
    orator 32, 73, 81, 138
    n.1
Aeschylus 26
  Prometheus Bound 75, 79, 143 n.6,
    144 n.11
Aesop 97
agon ('contest') 3, 43–52, 44
  and *anaideia* 45; *see also*
    anaidea
  and narrative of offstage
    action 65
  order of speakers 47
  and parodos 41
  pnigos 83, 144 n.12
  second 44, 70, 75–83
  and *tarattein* 80

and gifts 84, 105
and erotic rhetoric 125, 128,
  143 n.3
agora ('marketplace') 33, 129, *Fig.* 1
  and Agorakritos' name, *see under*
    Agorakritos
  and muster lists 127
  and narrative of offstage action
    63, 70
  and oracles 93, 111
Agorakritos
  characterization 26, 33, 39, 47, 66,
    67, 93, 139 n.7
  name 33, 111, 113
  trade 139 n.6
Amphipolis, *see under* Thucydides
anaideia (outrageousness) 45, 104,
    107–8, 141 n.1
  in the first agon 40, 44–5, 48, 49
  and Agorakritos 52, 66
  meaning 45
  and Paphlagon 46, 50
antepirrhema 44, 61
antistrophe 44, 60, 64, 75, 79, 86,
    119
Apollo
  oracles of 88, 94
    in Aristophanes 90
  authority of 32, 88, 90
  in *Cavalry* 32, 37, 90, 95–6,
    100
  and the Peloponnesian War 90
  shrine, at Delphi 88, 114, 119
archon, 38
  Basileus 4, 19–20
  eponymous 4
Areopagus 45, *Fig.* 1
Ariphrades, Athenian comic
    dramatist 115–19